WANDA E. BRUNSTETTER'S

Amish Friends

BAKING

COOKBOOK

Nearly 200 Delightful Baked Goods
Recipes from Amish Kitchens

BARBOUR

PUBLISHING

© 2021 by Wanda E. Brunstetter

Print ISBN 978-1-63609-085-6

All scripture quotations are taken from the King James Version of the Bible.

Published by Barbour Publishing, Inc., 1810 Barbour Drive, Uhrichsville, OH 44683, www.barbourbooks.com

Our mission is to inspire the world with the life-changing message of the Bible.

ecpa Member of the
Evangelical Christian
Publishers Association

Printed in China.

TABLE of CONTENTS

INTRODUCTION

When I was a young girl, my mother taught me how to bake cookies, cakes, cobblers, breads, muffins, and pies. One of my favorite recipes was for surprise muffins, which included a dollop of jelly in the center of each muffin before it was baked.

After I grew up, got married, and my daughter was old enough, I taught her how to bake. It was fun to create some of the baking recipes my mother had taught me and to know they were being handed down to the next generation.

I am now blessed with grandchildren, and I've had the privilege of passing on some family recipes to them as well. Since I am too busy writing to do much baking anymore, my youngest granddaughter will often come to my house and bake things for me.

My Amish friends are all good bakers, and many have shared their favorite recipes with me. Whenever my husband and I visit Amish country, we enjoy checking out some of the bakeries. I'm usually looking for baked goods that are gluten-free with small amounts of or no sugar. Since my husband grew up in Pennsylvania, one of his favorite treats is a chocolate or pumpkin whoopie pie.

I hope you will enjoy the recipes in this cookbook that are served in Amish homes to families who anticipate the tasty baked goods their mothers and grandmothers make for them.

A big thanks to my editor, Rebecca Germany, for all her help in putting this cookbook together.

"Give us this day our daily bread."
MATTHEW 6:11

Anabaptist History

T he Amish and Mennonites are direct descendants of the Anabaptists, a group that emerged from the Reformation in Switzerland in 1525 and developed separately in Holland a few years later. Most Anabaptists eventually became identified as Mennonites, after a prominent Dutch leader, Menno Simons. The word *Amish* comes from Jacob Ammann, an influential leader who in 1693 led a group that separated from the Mennonite churches. Driven by persecution from their homes in Switzerland and Germany, hundreds of Mennonites began to immigrate to North America, and in the 1700s the Amish sought homes in North America too. They were welcomed in Pennsylvania by William Penn and first settled there by the mid-nineteenth century.

As Amish communities continued to grow and seek more land, new Amish communities were started in other areas. Some moved to Ohio, Indiana, Iowa, and other parts of the country. Today there are Amish communities in many parts of the United States and Canada, and new ones continue to appear. The Amish population has grown to over two hundred thousand nationwide.

While all Amish adhere to the regulation of their *Ordnung* (church rules), many communities differ in practice, appearance, style of their homes, and types of buggies.

Both the Amish and Mennonites believe in the authority of the Scriptures, and their willingness to stand apart from the rest of the world shows through their simple, plain way of living.

Everywhere Amish settle, their baked goods are sought after at farmers' markets, flea markets, roadside stands, and bakeries.

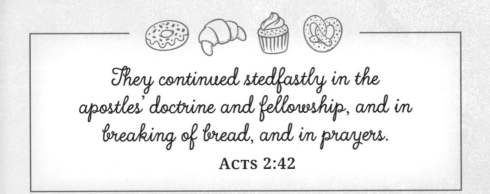

They continued stedfastly in the apostles' doctrine and fellowship, and in breaking of bread, and in prayers.

ACTS 2:42

COOKIES

*Often the first baked goods children will be encouraged
to help create in the kitchen are the little handheld treats
they love—cookies. An easy baking project they can get
their hands into, making cookies is a great event for
any family to bond over. And they are always
a welcome addition to a lunch box.*

Buttermilk Cookies

Emma Raber - *Holmesville, Ohio*

*This recipe won a first-place ribbon
at the Malheur County Fair in Ontario, Oregon.*

YIELDS

5 dozen cookies

INGREDIENTS:

2 cups butter or margarine,
   softened
3 cups brown sugar
1 cup sugar
3 eggs
4 teaspoons baking powder
4 teaspoons baking soda
4 teaspoons vanilla
1½ cups buttermilk or
   sour milk
8 cups flour

EQUIPMENT:

Large mixing bowl
Baking sheets
Spoons

INSTRUCTIONS:

1. Preheat oven to 350 degrees.

2. In mixing bowl, cream butter and sugars. Add eggs, baking powder, baking soda, and vanilla. Mix well. Add milk alternately with flour until well blended.

3. Drop by teaspoonfuls onto well-greased baking sheet.

4. Bake 11 to 13 minutes.

5. Let set for 5 minutes before removing from baking sheet.

SWEDISH BUTTER COOKIES

Linda E. Peachey - *Beaver, Ohio*

YIELDS

2 dozen cookies

INGREDIENTS:

1 cup butter, softened (no substitutes)
1 cup sugar
2 teaspoons maple syrup
2 cups flour
1 teaspoon baking soda

EQUIPMENT:

Large mixing bowl
Baking sheets
Spoon

INSTRUCTIONS:

1. Preheat oven to 300 degrees.

2. In mixing bowl, cream butter and sugar. Add maple syrup and stir well. Combine flour and baking soda. Add to creamed mixture.

3. Shape into balls and place on ungreased baking sheet.

4. Bake 25 minutes or until lightly browned.

Church Sugar Cookies

Mary K. Bontrager - *Middlebury, Indiana*

YIELDS
6 dozen cookies

INGREDIENTS:
1 cup sugar

2 cups brown sugar

2 cups vegetable oil

4 eggs, beaten

2 cups buttermilk or
  sour cream

1 tablespoon vanilla

1 (3 ounce) box instant
  vanilla pudding mix

2 tablespoons baking powder

½ teaspoon salt

2 teaspoons baking soda

6½ cups flour

Flour for dusting
  baking sheets

Sugar for sprinkling

EQUIPMENT:
Large mixing bowl

Spoons

Baking sheets

INSTRUCTIONS:

1. Preheat oven to 350 degrees.

2. In mixing bowl, cream sugars, oil, and eggs. Add buttermilk, then vanilla and pudding mix. Stir in remaining ingredients.

3. Sprinkle flour lightly onto baking sheet. Drop cookie dough by teaspoonfuls onto baking sheet. Sprinkle cookies generously with sugar.

4. Bake 12 to 14 minutes. Cookies are done when centers spring back when touched.

Measuring Tip

Some recipes call for a pinch or a dash of salt or other ingredient. Experienced cooks get a feel for what those mean, but a beginning cook could use this general reference:

Tad = ¼ teaspoon   Pinch = $\frac{1}{16}$ teaspoon

Dash = ⅛ teaspoon   Smidgen = $\frac{1}{32}$ teaspoon

Honey Sugar Cookies

Mary Wagler - *Montgomery, Indiana*

These are very chewy and delicious!

YIELDS
8 dozen cookies

INGREDIENTS:
2 cups sugar
2 cups brown sugar
2 cups butter, softened
1 cup shortening
1 cup honey
4 eggs
6 teaspoons baking soda
9 cups flour
1 teaspoon salt
1 cup sugar
2 teaspoons cinnamon

EQUIPMENT:
Large mixing bowl
Small bowl
Baking sheets
Spoon

INSTRUCTIONS:
1. Preheat oven to 350 degrees.

2. In large mixing bowl, cream 2 cups sugar, brown sugar, butter, and shortening. Add honey. Mix well. Add eggs. Beat. Work in baking soda, flour, and salt.

3. In small bowl, combine 1 cup sugar and cinnamon.

4. Shape dough into balls. Roll each ball in cinnamon-sugar mixture.

5. Bake on baking sheets 8 to 10 minutes until golden brown.

SNICKERDOODLES

VERNIE SCHWARTZ - *Stanwood, Michigan*

YIELDS
3 dozen cookies

INGREDIENTS:
2¾ cups flour
3 teaspoons baking powder
½ teaspoon salt
1½ cups sugar
1 cup butter or shortening, softened
2 eggs, beaten
4 teaspoons cinnamon
4 tablespoons sugar

EQUIPMENT:
Sifter
Mixing bowls
Small bowl
Baking sheets
Spoon

INSTRUCTIONS:
1. Preheat oven to 400 degrees.
2. Sift together flour, baking powder, and salt into mixing bowl.
3. In large mixing bowl, cream 1½ cups sugar and butter until fluffy. Add eggs and mix. Gradually add sifted mixture. Mix well. Chill.
4. Roll teaspoonfuls of dough into balls.
5. In small bowl, combine cinnamon and 4 tablespoons sugar and roll dough in mixture. Place balls 2 inches apart on ungreased baking sheet.
6. Bake 10 minutes.

Children's Delight Cookies

Susanna Miller - *Decatur, Indiana*

YIELDS

4 dozen cookies

INGREDIENTS:

1 cup sugar
1 cup brown sugar
1 cup shortening
2 eggs
1 teaspoon vanilla
2 cups flour
½ teaspoon salt
1 teaspoon baking soda
1 teaspoon baking powder
2 cups oats
½ cup chopped nuts
1 cup chocolate chips

EQUIPMENT:

Large mixing bowl
Baking sheets
Spoon

INSTRUCTIONS:

1. Preheat oven to 350 degrees.

2. Cream sugar, brown sugar, and shortening. Beat in eggs and vanilla. Add flour, salt, baking soda, and baking powder. Mix well. Stir in oats, nuts, and chocolate chips.

3. Drop by teaspoonfuls on baking sheet. Flatten slightly.

4. Bake 10 to 12 minutes. Cool.

5. Frost with your favorite frosting if desired.

Chocolate Crinkles

Martha Beechy - *Butler, Ohio*

YIELDS

4 dozen cookies

INGREDIENTS:

½ cup butter
2 cups sugar
4 eggs
2 teaspoons vanilla
4 cups flour
½ cup cocoa powder
2 teaspoons baking powder
½ teaspoon salt
Powdered sugar

EQUIPMENT:

Large mixing bowl
Baking sheets
Spoon

INSTRUCTIONS:

1. Preheat oven to 350 degrees.

2. In mixing bowl, mix butter, sugar, eggs, and vanilla. Add flour, cocoa, baking powder, and salt. Mix well and chill for several hours.

3. Form dough into balls and roll in powdered sugar. Place on baking sheet.

4. Bake 10 to 12 minutes or until done.

5. If desired, place cream filling sandwich style between cookies to make whoopie pies.

CLASSIC CHOCOLATE CHIP COOKIES

JONAS AND SARAH GINGERICH - *Junction City, Ohio*

These are a good seller at our produce and bake stand.

YIELDS
10 dozen cookies

INGREDIENTS:
4 cups butter
1 cup sugar
3 cups brown sugar
8 eggs
4 teaspoons vanilla
4 (6.5 ounce) boxes instant vanilla pudding mix
9 cups flour
4 teaspoons baking soda
1 teaspoon baking powder
4 cups chocolate chips

EQUIPMENT:
Large mixing bowl
Baking sheets
Spoon

INSTRUCTIONS:
1. Preheat oven to 375 degrees.
2. In larger mixing bowl, cream butter, sugars, eggs, and vanilla. Add and mix remaining ingredients.
3. Drop by teaspoonfuls onto baking sheets.
4. Bake 9 minutes.

DOUBLE TREAT COOKIES

SARAH DF SCHWARTZ - *Galesburg, Kansas*

YIELDS
4 dozen cookies

INGREDIENTS:
1 cup peanut butter
1 cup shortening
2 cups white or brown sugar
2 eggs
2 cups flour
2 teaspoons baking soda
½ teaspoon salt
1 cup chopped nuts
1 cup chocolate chips

EQUIPMENT:
Mixing bowl
Spoon
Baking sheets

INSTRUCTIONS:

1. Preheat oven to 350 degrees.

2. In mixing bowl, cream peanut butter, shortening, and sugar. Mix in eggs. Add flour, baking soda, and salt. Fold in nuts and chocolate chips.

3. Shape dough into balls. Place on baking sheet. Flatten with glass dipped in sugar.

4. Bake 10 to 12 minutes.

Simple Peanut Butter Oatmeal Cookies

Phebe Peight - *McVeytown, Pennsylvania*

YIELDS

2 dozen cookies

INGREDIENTS:

⅔ cup peanut butter (may
substitute almond or
cashew butter)

½ cup molasses or honey

2 teaspoons vanilla

2 cups oats

EQUIPMENT:

Mixing bowl
Spoon
Baking sheets

INSTRUCTIONS:

1. Preheat oven to 350 degrees.

2. In bowl, mix peanut butter and molasses until smooth. Stir in vanilla and oats.

3. Form into balls and place on greased baking sheet. Flatten.

4. Bake 8 to 9 minutes.

Espresso Cookies

Malachi and Ida Mae Stauffer - *Homer City, Pennsylvania*

YIELDS

3 dozen cookies

INGREDIENTS:

1 cup butter, softened
6 tablespoons sugar
2 cups brown sugar
2 large eggs
4 teaspoons vanilla
3½ cups flour
1 teaspoon baking powder
1 teaspoon baking soda
1 tablespoon instant coffee
2 cups chocolate chips

EQUIPMENT:

Mixing bowl
Spoon
Baking sheets

INSTRUCTIONS:

1. Preheat oven to 375 degrees.

2. In mixing bowl, cream butter, sugar, and brown sugar. Beat in eggs and vanilla. Stir in flour, baking powder, baking soda, and coffee. Fold in chocolate chips.

3. Bake 10 to 12 minutes. Don't overbake.

Pumpkin Cookies

RHONDA ROPP - *Crofton, Kentucky*

YIELDS
2½ dozen cookies

COOKIE INGREDIENTS:
1 cup sugar
½ cup butter
1 egg
1 teaspoon vanilla
1 cup pumpkin puree
2 cups flour
1 teaspoon baking soda
½ teaspoon baking powder
1 teaspoon cinnamon
¼ teaspoon salt

FROSTING INGREDIENTS:
3 tablespoons butter
4 tablespoons milk
½ cup brown sugar
Powdered sugar
1 teaspoon vanilla

EQUIPMENT:
2 mixing bowls
Spoon
Baking sheets
Parchment paper
Small saucepan

TO MAKE COOKIES:
1. Preheat oven to 350 degrees.
2. In mixing bowl, cream sugar and butter. Add egg, vanilla, and pumpkin. Mix well.
3. In another bowl, combine flour, baking soda, baking powder, cinnamon, and salt. Add to pumpkin mixture.
4. Drop dough by teaspoonfuls on parchment-lined baking sheet.
5. Bake 12 to 15 minutes.
6. Cool and frost.

TO MAKE FROSTING:
1. In saucepan, boil butter, milk, and brown sugar 2 minutes.
2. Let cool and add powdered sugar and vanilla.
3. Spread on cookies. Will be thin but will thicken as it cools on the cookies.

Old-Fashioned Ginger Cookies

RUTH S. MARTIN - *Selinsgrove, Pennsylvania*

YIELDS

8 dozen cookies

INGREDIENTS:

2 cups molasses

1 cup sugar

2 cups shortening

10 cups flour (half pastry and half bread flour)

1 teaspoon salt

2 tablespoons baking soda

1 teaspoon ginger

1 teaspoon cinnamon

2 cups sour milk or buttermilk

1 egg

EQUIPMENT:

Small saucepan

Sifter

Mixing bowl

Spoon

Small bowl

Baking sheets

Pastry brush

INSTRUCTIONS:

1. Preheat oven to 350 degrees.

2. In saucepan, heat molasses and sugar. Add shortening and stir until smooth. Remove from heat.

3. Sift together flour, salt, baking soda, ginger, and cinnamon in bowl. Add to molasses mixture alternately with milk. Stir until smooth dough forms. Work with hands 5 minutes. Chill.

4. Roll out to ½ inch thick and cut into shapes.

5. In small bowl, beat egg. Glaze cookies with egg.

6. Bake on greased baking sheet 20 to 25 minutes.

For Fluffy Cookies

For lighter, fluffier cookies, use vegetable shortening in place of butter.

MAPLE NUT COOKIES

LIZZIE YODER - *Fredericksburg, Ohio*

YIELDS

4 dozen cookies

COOKIE INGREDIENTS:

2 cups brown sugar

1 cup butter

3 eggs

1¼ tablespoons maple flavoring

¾ cup milk

4 cups flour

2 teaspoons baking soda

¼ teaspoon salt

¾ cup chopped nuts

FROSTING INGREDIENTS:

¼ cup butter

2¼ cups powdered sugar, divided

1 egg, beaten

1 teaspoon maple flavoring

2 teaspoons water

EQUIPMENT:

2 mixing bowls

Spoon

Baking sheets

TO MAKE COOKIES:

1. Preheat oven to 350 degrees.

2. In bowl, cream brown sugar and butter. Add eggs, maple flavoring, and milk. Beat well.

3. In separate bowl, combine flour, baking soda, and salt. Add to creamed mixture. Fold in nuts.

4. Drop by heaping teaspoonfuls onto greased baking sheet.

5. Bake 8 to 10 minutes.

6. Cool and frost.

TO MAKE FROSTING:

Beat butter until soft. Gradually add 1 cup powdered sugar. Add egg and maple flavoring, blending well. Add remaining sugar alternately with water until of spreading consistency.

Molasses Crème Cookies

Jolene Bontrager - *Topeka, Indiana*

YIELDS
115 sandwich cookies

COOKIE INGREDIENTS:
2¾ cups shortening
5 cups brown sugar
4 eggs
1 cup light molasses
1 cup milk
4 teaspoons cinnamon
⅛ teaspoon salt
2 teaspoons baking powder
8 teaspoons baking soda
10 cups flour
2 cups whole wheat flour

FILLING INGREDIENTS:
½ cup butter, softened
1 (8 ounce) package cream cheese, softened
1 teaspoon vanilla
⅛ teaspoon salt
1 tablespoon milk
1 tablespoon flour
6 cups powdered sugar

EQUIPMENT:
2 large mixing bowls
Spoon
Small bowl
Baking sheets

TO MAKE COOKIES:

1. Preheat oven to 350 degrees.
2. In large bowl, cream shortening and brown sugar. Add eggs, molasses, and milk.
3. In separate bowl, mix cinnamon, salt, baking powder, baking soda, flour, and wheat flour.
4. Slowly combine wet and dry mixtures.
5. Chill dough 8 hours or overnight.
6. Shape into 1-inch balls. Roll in white sugar. Flatten slightly.
7. Bake 8 to 10 minutes. Do not overbake.
8. Cool completely before assembling sandwich style with cream cheese filling.
9. These cookies store well in freezer for several months.

TO MAKE FILLING:

In bowl, cream butter and cream cheese. Add vanilla, salt, milk, and flour. Work in powdered sugar and mix until creamy.

PUMPKIN WHOOPIE PIES

FROM *Amish Cooking Class Cookbook*

YIELDS

18 cookies

COOKIE INGREDIENTS:

2 cups brown sugar

1 cup vegetable oil

1½ cups pumpkin (cooked or canned)

2 eggs

1 teaspoon vanilla

3 cups flour

1 teaspoon salt

1 teaspoon baking powder

1 teaspoon baking soda

1½ tablespoons cinnamon

½ tablespoon ginger

½ tablespoon cloves

FILLING INGREDIENTS:

2 egg whites

1½ cups shortening

1 teaspoon vanilla

¼ teaspoon salt

4½ cups powdered sugar

EQUIPMENT:

2 mixing bowls

Spoon

Baking sheets

Handheld mixer

Knife or spatula

Plastic wrap

TO MAKE COOKIES:

1. Preheat oven to 350 degrees.

2. Cream sugar and oil in mixing bowl. Add pumpkin, eggs, and vanilla. Mix well. Add dry ingredients and stir until combined.

3. Drop by heaping teaspoonfuls onto greased baking sheet. Bake 10 to 12 minutes.

TO MAKE FILLING:

1. In bowl, beat egg whites with mixer and add shortening, vanilla, and salt until well combined. Stir in powdered sugar and mix until creamy.

2. Spread filling sandwich style between cookies. Wrap each "sandwich" in plastic wrap.

Oatmeal Whoopie Pies

Lena Bender - *McVeytown, Pennsylvania*

YIELDS

2 dozen cookies

COOKIE INGREDIENTS:

¾ cup butter

2 cups brown sugar

2 eggs

2 cups flour

½ teaspoon salt

1 teaspoon baking powder

2 cups quick cooking oats

1 teaspoon cinnamon

2 teaspoons baking soda

3 tablespoons boiling water

FILLING INGREDIENTS:

5 tablespoons flour

1 cup milk

1 cup powdered sugar

½ teaspoon vanilla

¼ cup margarine

¼ cup shortening

EQUIPMENT:

Mixing bowl

Spoon

Baking sheets

Small saucepan

Spatula or knife

TO MAKE COOKIES:

1. Preheat oven to 325 degrees.

2. In mixing bowl, cream butter, sugar, and eggs. Combine flour, salt, and baking powder, and add to creamed mixture. Stir in oats and cinnamon.

3. Stir baking soda into boiling water. Add to batter and blend well.

4. Drop by tablespoonfuls onto greased baking sheet.

5. Bake 10 to 15 minutes.

6. Cool and spread filling sandwich style between cookies.

TO MAKE FILLING:

1. Cook flour and milk until mixture forms smooth paste. Cool.

2. Add powdered sugar, vanilla, margarine, and shortening, and beat until mixture resembles whipped cream.

3. Spread filling sandwich style between cookies.

Note: These are best frozen and eaten directly from the freezer.

Raisin-Filled Cookies

Velma Schrock - *Goshen, Indiana*

Dough needs to chill overnight.

YIELDS

5 dozen cookies

DOUGH INGREDIENTS:

2 cups shortening (can use half butter)

2 cups sugar

1 cup brown sugar

4 eggs

2 tablespoons milk

7 cups flour

2 teaspoons baking soda

1 teaspoon salt

2 teaspoons vanilla

FILLING INGREDIENTS:

4 cups raisins

2 cups water

1 cup sugar

2 teaspoons vinegar

2 tablespoons flour

2 teaspoons vanilla

1 cup chopped nuts

EQUIPMENT:

Mixing bowl

Small mixing bowl

Wax paper

Saucepan

Spoons

Baking sheets

Parchment paper

TO MAKE DOUGH:

1. In large mixing bowl, cream shortening and sugars.
2. In separate bowl, beat eggs with milk and add to creamed mixture.
3. Add dry ingredients and vanilla. Mix well.
4. Shape into 2-inch-thick rolls, wrap in wax paper, and chill overnight.

TO MAKE FILLING:

In saucepan, cook all ingredients until raisins are soft. Cool.

ASSEMBLY INSTRUCTIONS:

1. Preheat oven to 350 degrees.
2. Cut cookie dough into ⅛-inch slices. Place 1 tablespoon filling in middle of dough slice and cover with another slice. As cookie bakes, top slice will seal to bottom.
3. Bake on parchment-lined baking sheets 15 minutes or until lightly browned.

Note: These keep well in the freezer.

Date Pinwheel Cookies

Susan Weaver - *Osseo, Michigan*

Filling and dough need to be thoroughly chilled before assembly.
Chilling overnight before baking is recommended.

YIELDS

4 dozen cookies

FILLING INGREDIENTS:

2 pounds chopped dates
1 cup sugar
1 cup water

DOUGH INGREDIENTS:

1⅓ cups brown sugar
⅔ cup shortening
2 eggs, beaten
2½ cups flour
¾ teaspoon baking soda
½ teaspoon salt
½ teaspoon cinnamon

EQUIPMENT:

Saucepan
Spoons
2 mixing bowls
Wax paper and/or plastic wrap
Sharp knife
Baking sheets

TO MAKE FILLING:

Combine dates, sugar, and water in saucepan. Cook over medium-low heat, stirring constantly until mixture forms smooth paste. Cool.

TO MAKE DOUGH:

1. In large bowl, cream brown sugar and shortening. Add eggs and beat until mixture is light and fluffy.

2. In separate bowl, combine flour, baking soda, salt, and cinnamon. Gradually add to creamed mixture and stir until soft dough forms.

3. Divide dough into 4 parts. Cover with wax paper and chill thoroughly.

ASSEMBLY INSTRUCTIONS:

1. Working with one portion of dough at a time while keeping remaining dough cool, roll out rectangle ⅛ inch thick.

2. Spread date filling to within ¼ inch of edges. Roll up jelly roll style, starting with long side. Pinch edge to seal.

3. Wrap each roll in wax paper or plastic wrap and refrigerate overnight.

4. Preheat oven to 400 degrees.

5. Remove rolls from refrigerator. With sharp knife, cut in ¼-inch slices and place on lightly greased baking sheet.

6. Bake 8 to 10 minutes or until light golden brown.

FRUIT COOKIES

MRS. TOBY (MERIAM) BYLER - *Watsontown, Pennsylvania*
MARY STUTZMAN - *West Salem, Ohio*

YIELDS
4 dozen cookies

INGREDIENTS:
½ cup chopped apple
½ cup chopped dates
1 cup raisins
1 cup water
⅓ cup vegetable oil
3 eggs
½ teaspoon salt
1⅓ cups whole wheat flour
or 1½ cups white flour
1 teaspoon vanilla
1 teaspoon baking soda
1 teaspoon cinnamon
½ cup chopped walnuts

EQUIPMENT:
Large saucepan
Spoon
Baking sheets

INSTRUCTIONS:
1. Preheat oven to 350 degrees.
2. In saucepan, cook apples, dates, and raisins in water for 3 minutes. Cool. Add oil, eggs, salt, flour, vanilla, baking soda, and cinnamon Mix well. Stir in walnuts.
3. Dough can be chilled before baking.
4. Drop on greased baking sheet.
5. Bake 15 minutes. Do not overbake.
6. Store in cold place.

Go thy way, eat thy bread with joy!

ECCLESIASTES 9:7

BARS

*Bar treats are an easy way to make a quick handheld dessert
for an event like Sunday potluck or unexpected company.
Layers of goodness are packed into a single pan.
Bars can be cut into oblongs, squares, or diamonds.*

Speedy Brownies

Martha Petersheim - *Junction City, Ohio*

These are simple and easy to make. Ideal to take along to a finger-food dinner or a picnic.

YIELDS

3 dozen small bars

INGREDIENTS:

2 cups sugar

½ cup cocoa powder

5 eggs

1 teaspoon vanilla

1¾ cups flour

1 teaspoon salt

1 cup vegetable oil

1 cup semisweet chocolate chips

EQUIPMENT:

Mixing bowl

Spoon

9x13-inch pan

Toothpick

INSTRUCTIONS:

1. Preheat oven to 350 degrees.

2. In mixing bowl, combine all ingredients except for chocolate chips. Beat until smooth.

3. Pour batter into greased 9x13-inch pan. Sprinkle with chocolate chips.

4. Bake 30 minutes or until toothpick inserted near center comes out clean. Cool on wire rack.

ZUCCHINI BROWNIES

MRS. ANDY L. SCHLABACH - *Spencer, Ohio*

YIELDS
3 dozen bars

INGREDIENTS:
4 eggs
1½ cups vegetable oil
2 cups sugar
2 cups flour
2 teaspoons baking soda
2 teaspoons cinnamon
1 teaspoon salt
4 tablespoons cocoa powder
1 teaspoon vanilla
4 cups shredded zucchini
1 cup chopped nuts

EQUIPMENT:
Mixing bowl
Handheld mixer
Sifter
Spoon
10x15-inch jelly roll pan

INSTRUCTIONS:
1. Preheat oven to 350 degrees.
2. In bowl, use mixer to beat eggs, oil, and sugar.
3. In separate bowl, sift together flour, baking soda, cinnamon, salt, and cocoa. Add to egg mixture and blend well. Stir in vanilla, zucchini, and nuts.
4. Spread in greased and floured 10x15-inch jelly roll pan. Bake 30 minutes.
5. Serve plain or frosted.

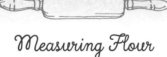

Measuring Flour

Flour packs down, so your method of measuring can affect the accuracy of your measurement and change the outcome of your recipe. To start, use a spoon to stir the flour in your storage container that has sat and settled. Then use the spoon to gently fill your measuring cup. Use a flat edge like a knife to level off the top of the cup's contents and push the excess back into the flour bin. If the recipe calls for sifted flour, measure out the listed amount, then sift it. If you don't have a flour sifter, you can put the flour into a strainer and shake it into your mixing bowl. You can also sift or fluff your flour with a whisk or fork if necessary.

Apple Butter Bars

Nelson and Miriam Hershberger - *Calhoun, Illinois*

YIELDS

24 bars

INGREDIENTS:

1½ cups flour
1 teaspoon baking soda
1 teaspoon salt
2½ cups quick oats
1½ cups sugar
1 cup margarine, softened
1½ cups apple butter

EQUIPMENT:

Sifter
Mixing bowl
9x13-inch pan
Spoon

INSTRUCTIONS:

1. Preheat oven to 350 degrees.

2. Sift flour, baking soda, and salt into large bowl. Add oats and sugar. Stir in margarine and mix well.

3. Press half of mixture into greased 9x13-inch pan. Top with apple butter. Sprinkle with remaining crumbs and press gently with spoon.

4. Bake 55 minutes or until lightly browned.

BUTTERSCOTCH CHEESE BARS

SHARON ZIMMERMAN - *Port Trevorton, Pennsylvania*

YIELDS

24 bars

INGREDIENTS:

⅓ cup butter

8 ounces butterscotch chips

2 cups graham cracker crumbs

1 cup nuts, chopped

1 (8 ounce) package cream cheese, softened

1 egg

1 teaspoon vanilla

1 can (14 ounces) sweetened condensed milk

EQUIPMENT:

Microwaveable bowl or double broiler

Greased 9x13-inch pan

Mixing bowl

Handheld mixer

Spoon or spatula

INSTRUCTIONS:

1. Preheat oven to 350 degrees.

2. Melt butter and butterscotch chips in microwaveable bowl or in double boiler.

3. Add graham cracker crumbs and nuts. Mix well and press half of crumb mixture into greased 9x13-inch pan.

4. In mixing bowl, beat cream cheese, egg, vanilla, and condensed milk, and pour over crumbs. Sprinkle reserved crumbs on top.

5. Bake 25 to 30 minutes.

Cherry Melt-Away Bars

Mattie Yoder - *Fairchild, Wisconsin*

YIELDS

24 bars

INGREDIENTS:

2 cups flour

2 eggs, separated

1½ cups sugar, divided

1 cup margarine or butter

2 cans or 1 quart cherry
  pie filling

Dash cream of tartar

1 teaspoon vanilla

½ cup chopped nuts

EQUIPMENT:

Mixing bowl

9x13-inch pan

Spoon

INSTRUCTIONS:

1. Preheat oven to 350 degrees.

2. In mixing bowl, combine flour, egg yolks, 1 cup sugar, and margarine. Press into 9x13-inch pan. Spread pie filling on crust.

3. In clean bowl, beat egg whites with cream of tartar until stiff peaks form. Gradually beat in ½ cup sugar then vanilla. Spread over pie filling. Sprinkle with nuts.

4. Bake 30 to 35 minutes.

Chocolate Chip Cheesecake Bars

ABNER AND AMANDA MILLER - *Wisconsin Rapids, Wisconsin*

YIELDS

36 bars

CRUST INGREDIENTS:

¾ cup shortening
¾ cup sugar
⅓ cup brown sugar
1 egg
1½ teaspoons vanilla
1½ cups flour
1 teaspoon salt
¾ teaspoon baking soda
1½ cups chocolate chips
¾ cup chopped walnuts

FILLING INGREDIENTS:

2 (8 ounce) packages cream cheese
¾ cup sugar
2 eggs
1 teaspoon vanilla

EQUIPMENT:

3 mixing bowls
9x13-inch pan
Handheld mixer
Spoons

TO MAKE CRUST:

1. Preheat oven to 350 degrees.

2. In mixing bowl, cream shortening, sugar, and brown sugar. Beat in egg and vanilla.

3. In separate bowl, combine flour, salt, and baking soda. Add to creamed mixture and mix well. Fold in chocolate chips and nuts.

4. Set aside a third of dough for topping. Press remaining dough into greased 9x13-inch pan.

5. Bake 8 minutes.

TO MAKE FILLING:

1. Meanwhile, in clean bowl, beat cream cheese and sugar until smooth. Add eggs and vanilla. Mix well.

2. Spoon over hot crust. Drop teaspoonfuls of reserved dough over filling.

3. Bake 35 to 40 minutes until golden brown. Cool.

CHOCOLATE OATMEAL BARS

MARTHA PETERSHEIM - *Junction City, Ohio*

YIELDS

18 bars

INGREDIENTS:

½ cup butter, softened

½ cup brown sugar

1 egg

1 teaspoon vanilla

½ cup flour

½ cup quick oats

1 cup semisweet chocolate chips

½ cup chopped pecans

EQUIPMENT:

Mixing bowl

Handheld mixer

7x11-inch pan

Spatula

INSTRUCTIONS:

1. Preheat oven to 375 degrees.

2. In mixing bowl, use mixer to cream butter and brown sugar. Beat in egg and vanilla. Add flour and oats. Mix well.

3. Pour into lightly greased 7x11-inch baking pan.

4. Bake 15 to 20 minutes or until lightly browned. Cool on wire rack 3 to 5 minutes.

5. Sprinkle with chocolate chips. When chips are melted, spread over bars. Top with pecans.

COOKIE SHEET WHOOPIES

EMMA ZOOK - *Navarre, Ohio*

YIELDS
36 bars

INGREDIENTS:
1½ cups margarine

3½ cups sugar

4 eggs

2 teaspoons vanilla

4 cups flour

1½ cups cocoa powder

2½ teaspoons baking soda

1 teaspoon salt

2⅔ cups water

1 batch of whoopie pie filling (see page 26)

EQUIPMENT:
Mixing bowl

Handheld mixer

2 (10x15-inch) jelly roll pans

Spatula

INSTRUCTIONS:

1. Preheat oven to 375 degrees.

2. In mixing bowl, use mixer to cream margarine and sugar. Beat in eggs and vanilla. Mix in flour, cocoa, baking soda, and salt. Gradually add water. Mix well.

3. Divide dough in half and spread in 2 greased 10x15-inch baking pans.

4. Bake 20 to 25 minutes until done. Cool.

5. Top one cake with your choice of whoopie pie filling, then top with other cake. Cut into squares.

Fudge Nut Bars

Emma Zook - *Navarre, Ohio*

YIELDS
40 bars

DOUGH INGREDIENTS:

1 cup butter

2 cups brown sugar

2 eggs, beaten

2 teaspoons vanilla

2 cups flour

1 teaspoon baking soda

1 teaspoon salt

3 cups quick oats

FILLING INGREDIENTS:

2 tablespoons butter

1 cup chocolate chips

1 can sweetened condensed milk

½ teaspoon salt

1 cup nuts

2 teaspoons vanilla

EQUIPMENT:

Mixing bowl

Spoons

10x15-inch jelly roll pan

Small saucepan

TO MAKE DOUGH:

1. Preheat oven to 350 degrees.

2. In bowl, cream butter and brown sugar. Add eggs and vanilla. Add flour, baking soda, and salt. Mix well. Stir in oats.

3. Spread two-thirds of dough in 10x15-inch jelly roll pan.

TO MAKE FILLING:

1. In saucepan, combine butter, chocolate chips, milk, and salt. Stir until melted. Add nuts and vanilla.

2. Cover dough with chocolate filling. Top with remaining dough.

3. Bake 25 to 30 minutes.

Honey Bun Bars

Martha Miller - *Gallipolis, Ohio*

YIELDS

40 bars

BATTER INGREDIENTS:

3 eggs, separated

1½ cups sugar, divided

2¼ cups sifted flour

3 teaspoons baking powder

1 teaspoon salt

⅓ cup vegetable oil

1 cup water

1 teaspoon vanilla

3½ tablespoons sucanat or brown sugar

2½ teaspoons cinnamon

FROSTING INGREDIENTS:

¼ cup butter

⅓ scant cup sucanat

⅛ cup water

3 ounces cream cheese

½ teaspoon vanilla

EQUIPMENT:

2 mixing bowls

Small bowl

Handheld mixer

Sifter

Spoons

10x15-inch jelly roll pan

Small saucepan

TO MAKE BATTER:

1. Preheat oven to 350 degrees.

2. In bowl, beat egg whites until frothy. Gradually add ½ cup sugar. Beat until stiff and glossy.

3. In another bowl, sift remaining sugar, flour, baking powder, and salt. Add oil, water, egg yolks, and vanilla. Beat until smooth. Fold in egg whites.

4. Pour half of batter into 10x15-inch jelly roll pan.

5. In small bowl, combine sucanat and cinnamon and sprinkle over top batter. Add remaining batter.

6. Bake 40 minutes.

TO MAKE FROSTING:

1. In saucepan, brown butter for 5 minutes.

2. Add sucanat and water. Cook 5 minutes.

3. Remove from heat and add cream cheese and vanilla, beating until smooth.

4. Spread on top of bars.

LEMON BARS

EMMA E. RABER - *Holmesville, Ohio*

YIELDS
36 bars

CRUST INGREDIENTS:
1 cup butter or margarine
2 cups flour
½ cup powdered sugar
Pinch salt

FILLING INGREDIENTS:
4 eggs, beaten
2 cups sugar
6 tablespoons lemon juice
4 tablespoons flour
¼ to ½ cup powdered sugar

EQUIPMENT:
2 mixing bowls
Spoons
Handheld mixer
9x13-inch pan

TO MAKE CRUST:

1. Preheat oven to 350 degrees.

2. In bowl, mix butter, flour, powdered sugar, and salt. Pat into 9x13-inch pan.

3. Bake 15 to 20 minutes.

TO MAKE FILLING:

1. In bowl, beat eggs, sugar, lemon juice, and flour.

2. Pour over baked crust and bake 20 to 30 minutes more.

3. Sprinkle powdered sugar lightly over top after removing from oven.

Maple Chocolate Walnut Bars

Alice Beechy - *Pittsford, Michigan*

YIELDS

24 bars

CRUST INGREDIENTS:

1½ cups flour

⅔ cup sugar

¾ cup cold butter or margarine

½ teaspoon salt

1 egg, beaten

FILLING INGREDIENTS:

1 cup chocolate chips

1 (14 ounce) can sweetened condensed milk

1½ teaspoons maple flavoring

1 egg, beaten

2 cups walnuts, chopped

EQUIPMENT:

2 mixing bowls

Spoons

9x13-inch pan

TO MAKE CRUST:

1. Preheat oven to 350 degrees.

2. In large bowl, mix flour, sugar, butter, and salt until crumbly. Stir in beaten egg. Press evenly into greased 9x13-inch pan.

3. Bake 25 minutes.

TO MAKE FILLING:

1. Sprinkle chocolate chips over hot baked crust.

2. In bowl, combine condensed milk, flavoring, and egg. Stir in walnuts. Pour over chocolate chips.

3. Return to oven to bake 20 minutes longer or until golden brown.

4. Cool. Cut into bars.

Don't overlook life's small joys while searching for the big ones.

MONSTER COOKIE BARS

DAVID L. BYLER - *New Wilmington, Pennsylvania*

YIELDS

40 bars

INGREDIENTS:

½ cup margarine or butter, melted

1½ cups creamy peanut butter

1 cup sugar

1¼ cups brown sugar

3 eggs

1 teaspoon corn syrup

4 cups oats

2 teaspoons baking soda

1 cup M&M's

¾ cup chocolate chips

EQUIPMENT:

Mixing bowl

Spoon

10x15-inch jelly roll pan (9x13-inch pan will also work for thicker bars)

INSTRUCTIONS:

1. Preheat oven to 350 degrees.

2. Mix all ingredients in order given. Spread in jelly roll pan.

3. Bake 15 to 20 minutes. Do not overbake.

Note: Dough may be used for cookies instead of bars.

OATMEAL RAISIN BARS

DOROTHY YODER - *Scottville, Michigan*

YIELDS
40 bars

INGREDIENTS:
1 cup butter, softened
1 cup sugar
1 cup brown sugar
2 eggs
2 teaspoons vanilla
2 cups flour
2 cups oats
1 teaspoon baking powder
1 teaspoon baking soda
1 teaspoon salt
1 cup raisins or dried
   cranberries
1 cup shredded coconut
1 cup butterscotch or
   white chips

EQUIPMENT:
Mixing bowl
Spoon
10x15-inch jelly roll pan

INSTRUCTIONS:
1. Preheat oven to 350 degrees.
2. In bowl, blend butter, sugar, and brown sugar. Add eggs and vanilla. Blend in flour, oats, baking powder, baking soda, and salt. Stir in raisins, coconut, and butterscotch chips.
3. Spread in 10x15-inch jelly roll pan.
4. Bake 15 minutes.

PECAN SQUARES

MARY SCHWARTZ - *Monroe, Indiana*

YIELDS

2 dozen squares

CRUST INGREDIENTS:

3 cups flour

½ cup sugar

1 cup butter or margarine, softened

½ teaspoon salt

FILLING INGREDIENTS:

4 eggs

1½ cups light or dark corn syrup

1½ cups sugar

3 tablespoons butter or margarine, melted

1½ teaspoons vanilla

2½ cups chopped pecans

EQUIPMENT:

2 mixing bowls

Spoon

9x13-inch pan

Knife or spatula

TO MAKE CRUST:

1. Preheat oven to 350 degrees.

2. In mixing bowl, blend flour, sugar, butter, and salt until mixture forms coarse crumbs. Press into greased 9x13-inch pan.

3. Bake 20 minutes.

TO MAKE FILLING:

1. While crust bakes, combine eggs, corn syrup, sugar, butter, and vanilla. Stir in pecans.

2. Spread filling evenly over hot crust and bake 25 minutes longer or until set.

3. Cool and cut into squares. Store in airtight container.

Muffin Tin Cookie Bowls

Want to make cookie bowls for your next ice cream sundae? Flip a muffin tin upside down and mold cookie dough over the bottom of each cup. Bake according to cookie recipe and well browned.

Peanut Butter Fingers

Amanda Stutzman - *Apple Creek, Ohio*

YIELDS

24 bars

DOUGH INGREDIENTS:

½ cup butter or margarine

½ cup white sugar

½ cup brown sugar

1 egg

⅓ cup peanut butter

½ teaspoon baking soda

¼ teaspoon salt

½ teaspoon vanilla

1 cup rolled oats

1 cup flour

1 (6 ounce) package chocolate chips

FROSTING INGREDIENTS:

½ cup powdered sugar

¼ cup peanut butter

2 to 4 tablespoons milk

EQUIPMENT:

2 mixing bowls

Spoon

9x13-inch pan

Knife or spatula

TO MAKE DOUGH:

1. Preheat oven to 350 degrees.

2. In bowl, cream butter and sugars. Blend in egg and peanut butter. Add baking soda, salt, vanilla, oats, and flour. Mix well.

3. Bake in greased 9x13-inch pan 20 to 25 minutes.

4. Spread chocolate chips over the top while still hot. Cool.

5. Frost with Peanut Butter Frosting. Cut into bars for serving.

TO MAKE FROSTING:

In bowl, combine powdered sugar and peanut butter. Stir in milk until it reaches the desired spreading consistency.

Pumpkin Bars

Martha Miller - *Gallipolis, Ohio*

YIELDS

40 bars

INGREDIENTS:

4 eggs
1 cup vegetable oil
2 cups sugar
1 cup canned pumpkin
½ teaspoon salt
2 teaspoons cinnamon
1 teaspoon baking soda
2 teaspoons baking powder
2 cups flour

EQUIPMENT:

Mixing bowl
Handheld mixer
10x15-inch jelly roll pan

INSTRUCTIONS:

1. Preheat oven to 350 degrees.
2. In bowl, combine all ingredients, mixing well, and pour into greased jelly roll pan.
3. Bake 20 to 25 minutes.

Soft Zucchini Bars

Judy Wengerd - *Monroe, Indiana*

YIELDS

3 dozen bars

BATTER INGREDIENTS:

2 cups sugar
1¼ cups vegetable oil
4 eggs
2 cups flour
2 teaspoons baking soda
1 teaspoon salt
1½ teaspoons cinnamon
2⅛ cups grated zucchini

FROSTING INGREDIENTS:

6 ounces cream cheese
¼ cup butter
2 teaspoons vanilla
1½ cups powdered sugar

EQUIPMENT:

2 mixing bowls
Spoon
10x15-inch jelly roll pan

TO MAKE BATTER:

1. Preheat oven to 350 degrees.
2. Mix sugar, oil, and eggs. Add flour, baking soda, salt, and cinnamon. Fold in zucchini.
3. Spread in greased jelly roll pan.
4. Bake 20 minutes.

TO MAKE FROSTING:

1. Combine ingredients and beat until smooth.
2. Spread over cooled bars.

SPICED GRANOLA BARS

JUDY ZIMMERMAN - *East Earl, Pennsylvania*

YIELDS

12 bars

INGREDIENTS:

1 cup gluten-free oats

¼ cup dried cranberries

¼ cup sunflower seeds

¼ cup shredded coconut

¼ cup chopped nuts

2 tablespoons cocoa powder

1 teaspoon cinnamon

1 teaspoon ginger

½ teaspoon salt

¾ cup applesauce

1 tablespoon blackstrap
   molasses

1½ teaspoons vanilla

EQUIPMENT:

Mixing bowl

Spoon

8x8-inch pan

INSTRUCTIONS:

1. Preheat oven to 325 degrees.

2. Combine all ingredients and pour into greased 8x8-inch pan.

3. Bake 15 to 17 minutes.

*Jesus said unto them, I am the bread of life:
he that cometh to me shall never hunger.*

JOHN 6:35

ENERGY BARS

VERNA STUTZMAN - *Navarre, Ohio*

YIELDS
40 bars

INGREDIENTS:
2 cups butter
3 cups brown sugar
⅔ cup molasses
⅔ cup peanut butter
4 large eggs
3 cups whole wheat flour
2 cups pastry flour
2 cups wheat germ
3 teaspoons baking soda
1 teaspoon salt
1 teaspoon cinnamon
4 cups quick oats
2 cups raisins
2 cups chocolate chips
2 cups chopped nuts

EQUIPMENT:
2 mixing bowls
Spoon
10x15-inch jelly roll pan

INSTRUCTIONS:
1. Preheat oven to 350 degrees.
2. In bowl, cream butter, brown sugar, molasses, and peanut butter. Add eggs.
3. In separate bowl, combine whole wheat flour, pastry flour, wheat germ, baking soda, salt, cinnamon, and oats. Add to creamed mixture. Stir in raisins, chocolate chips, and nuts. Spread in baking pan.
4. Bake 20 minutes.

Note: These can also be made into cookies.

CAKES

Cakes show up at all our special occasions, from birthdays to weddings. But cakes don't have to be elaborate, for the simplest supper or coffee cake can offer warmth and comfort to each guest at your table.

Easy Mix Chocolate Cake

Mrs. Samuel J. Schwartz - *Bryant, Indiana*

YIELDS
28 servings

CAKE INGREDIENTS:

3 cups flour

2 cups sugar

½ cup cocoa powder

½ teaspoon baking powder

2 teaspoons baking soda

1 cup hot water

1 cup lard

2 eggs

1 cup milk

ICING INGREDIENTS:

2 cups powdered sugar

½ cup cocoa powder

1 tablespoon creamy peanut
  butter

Water

EQUIPMENT:

2 mixing bowls

Spoon

10x15-inch jelly roll pan

Toothpick

Handheld mixer

INSTRUCTIONS:

1. Preheat oven to 350 degrees.

2. In mixing bowl, mix dry ingredients, then add remaining ingredients in order given. Pour batter into greased 10x15-inch jelly roll pan.

3. Bake 30 minutes or until toothpick inserted in center comes out clean. Cool.

4. Cover with icing.

TO MAKE ICING:

In bowl, combine powdered sugar and cocoa. Stir in peanut butter. Use mixer to beat with enough water to reach spreading consistency.

Easy Strawberry Shortcake

Susie Knepp - *Montgomery, Indiana*

YIELDS

9 servings

INGREDIENTS:

2 cups flour
1 cup sugar
⅓ cup butter
½ teaspoon baking soda
1 cup buttermilk
2 tablespoons sugar
1 tablespoon flour

EQUIPMENT:

Mixing bowl
Spoon
9x9-inch pan
Small bowl

INSTRUCTIONS:

1. Preheat oven to 350 degrees.

2. In large bowl, use spoon (not electric mixer) to combine 2 cups flour, 1 cup sugar, butter, baking soda, and buttermilk. Pour into greased 9x9-inch pan.

3. In small bowl, combine 2 tablespoons sugar and 1 tablespoon flour. Sprinkle over batter.

4. Bake 30 to 35 minutes.

5. Serve with fresh strawberries.

Dump Cake

Mrs. Andrew J. Hostetler - *Homerville, Ohio*

YIELDS

12 servings

INGREDIENTS:

1 cup cherry pie filling

1 can (15½ ounce) crushed pineapple, undrained

1 yellow cake mix

1 cup nuts, chopped

1 cup coconut, flaked

2 sticks margarine, melted

EQUIPMENT:

9x13-inch pan

INSTRUCTIONS:

1. Preheat oven to 350 degrees.
2. Spread pie filling and pineapple in ungreased 9x13-inch pan.
3. Sprinkle dry cake mix over fruit.
4. Top evenly with nuts and coconut.
5. Drizzle melted margarine over all.
6. Bake 70 minutes. Cool completely before cutting.

AMISH CAKE

ELIZABETH BYLER - *New Wilmington, Pennsylvania*

This is a good cake to make if eggs are scarce.

YIELDS
18 servings

BATTER INGREDIENTS:
½ cup butter
2 cups brown sugar
2 cups buttermilk or sour milk
2 teaspoons baking soda
3 cups flour
1 teaspoon vanilla

TOPPING INGREDIENTS:
6 tablespoons softened butter
4 tablespoons milk
1 cup brown sugar
½ cup nuts

EQUIPMENT:
Mixing bowl
Spoons
9x13-inch pan
Small bowl

TO MAKE BATTER:

1. Preheat oven to 375 degrees.

2. In bowl, cream butter and brown sugar.

3. Combine buttermilk with baking soda. Add to creamed mixture. Add flour and vanilla. Pour into greased and floured 9x13-inch pan.

4. Bake 30 minutes.

TO MAKE TOPPING:

1. While cake is baking, mix butter, milk, and brown sugar. Stir in nuts.

2. When cake is done, remove from oven and add topping.

3. Return cake to oven and bake 1 minute or until bubbly.

ANGEL FOOD CAKE

LYDIA MILLER - *Goshen, Indiana*

YIELDS

16 servings

CAKE INGREDIENTS:

2¼ cups egg whites, room temperature

¼ teaspoon salt

1½ teaspoons cream of tartar

1⅓ cups sugar

½ teaspoon almond flavoring or other flavoring

1½ cups cake flour

½ cup sugar

1 (3 ounce) box gelatin mix, any flavor (optional)

FROSTING INGREDIENTS:

1 (8 ounce) package cream cheese, softened

2 cups powdered sugar

1 cup heavy whipping cream

SAUCE INGREDIENTS:

1 tablespoon instant Clear Jel (can be found in bulk stores)

2 tablespoons sugar

1 pint strawberries, chopped

EQUIPMENT:

3 mixing bowls

Handheld mixer

Sifter

Spoons

Tube pan

Small bowl

TO MAKE CAKE:

1. Preheat oven to 375 degrees.

2. In mixing bowl, use mixer to beat egg whites, salt, and cream of tartar until stiff. Beat in 1⅓ cups sugar until it holds soft peaks. Fold in flavoring.

3. Sift together 1½ cups cake flour and ½ cup sugar, and fold into egg whites with spoon.

4. Optional: Add dry gelatin and fold in for nice color and different flavor.

5. In ungreased tube pan, bake 35 minutes. Cool completely before removing.

TO MAKE FROSTING:

1. In bowl, combine cream cheese and powdered sugar, and mix well.

2. In separate bowl, whip cream with mixer until stiff, then fold into cream cheese mixture.

3. Spread on cake.

TO MAKE SAUCE:

1. In small bowl, combine Clear Jel and sugar. Slowly add strawberries, stirring constantly. Do not heat.

2. When thickened, put sauce on top of frosted cake and let drip down sides.

3. Any thickened fruit may be used on top of cake.

CARROT CAKE
MRS. RAYMOND KAUFFMAN - *Laplata, Missouri*

YIELDS

18 servings

INGREDIENTS:

2 cups flour

1½ cups sugar

½ teaspoon salt

1 teaspoon cinnamon

1 teaspoon nutmeg

1 teaspoon ground cloves

½ teaspoon baking soda

1 teaspoon baking powder

¾ cup vegetable oil

4 eggs

3 cups grated carrots (can also use zucchini or sweet potatoes)

EQUIPMENT:

Mixing bowl

Spoons

9x13-inch pan (or use jelly roll pan for bars)

Small bowl

INSTRUCTIONS:

1. Preheat oven to 350 degrees.

2. In bowl, mix flour, sugar, salt, cinnamon, nutmeg, cloves, baking soda, and baking powder. Add oil and eggs, mixing well. Stir in carrots.

3. Pour into greased 9x13-inch pan.

4. Bake 45 minutes (30 minutes for bars in jelly roll pan).

5. Cool and frost with your favorite icing.

Feed your faith, and your doubts will starve to death.

CARAMEL APPLE CRUNCH CAKE

MARTHA YODER - *Harrisville, Pennsylvania*

YIELDS
16 servings

CAKE INGREDIENTS:
1½ cups vegetable oil
3 eggs
2 cups sugar
2 teaspoons vanilla
3 cups flour
1½ teaspoons baking soda
1 teaspoon salt
1 cup chopped walnuts
1 cup coconut
3 cups chopped apples

ICING INGREDIENTS:
½ cup (1 stick) butter
1 cup brown sugar
¼ cup milk

EQUIPMENT:
Large mixing bowl
Handheld mixer
Spoon
Tube pan
Serving plate
Small saucepan

TO MAKE CAKE:

1. Preheat oven to 350 degrees.

2. Using mixer, in mixing bowl, combine oil, eggs, sugar, and vanilla. Add flour, baking soda, and salt. Mix well. Stir in walnuts, coconut, and apples.

3. Pour into greased tube pan.

4. Bake 1½ hours.

5. Leave cake in pan until cool; then invert onto plate.

TO MAKE ICING:

1. Combine butter, brown sugar, and milk in saucepan. Boil 2½ minutes.

2. Drizzle hot icing over cake.

CHOCOLATE BEAN CAKE

MRS. PETER LANDIS - *Brodhead, Wisconsin*

A gluten-free treat!

YIELDS

12 servings

INGREDIENTS:

2 cups cooked beans of choice (black, pinto, navy), rinsed

6 eggs

¾ cup sugar or honey

1 teaspoon vanilla

¼ cup vegetable oil

½ cup cocoa powder

2 teaspoons baking powder

½ teaspoon salt

1 teaspoon baking soda

EQUIPMENT:

Blender or food processor

9x9-inch pan

INSTRUCTIONS:

1. Preheat oven to 350 degrees.

2. In blender or food processor, blend beans, eggs, sugar, and vanilla until thoroughly incorporated. Add oil, cocoa, baking powder, salt, and baking soda, mixing well.

3. Bake in greased 9x9-inch pan 25 to 30 minutes.

4. Frost if desired.

Cinnamon Roll Cake

Mrs. Emma Hochstetler - *Keytesville, Missouri*

YIELDS
18 servings

CAKE INGREDIENTS:
1½ cups brown sugar
1 cup butter, softened
2 eggs
1 cup milk
2 teaspoons vanilla
3 cups flour
3 teaspoons baking powder
1 teaspoon salt

SAUCE INGREDIENTS:
4 tablespoons butter, melted
1 cup brown sugar
2 to 4 teaspoons cinnamon
4 tablespoons flour
4 tablespoons water
1 cup nuts

GLAZE INGREDIENTS:
2 cups powdered sugar
2 tablespoons butter, melted
1 teaspoon vanilla
3 to 4 tablespoons milk

EQUIPMENT:
3 mixing bowls
Handheld mixer
9x13-inch pan
Small bowl

TO MAKE CAKE:

1. Preheat oven to 350 degrees.
2. In large bowl, use mixer to combine sugar and butter. Add eggs, milk, and vanilla. Slowly incorporate flour, baking powder, and salt. Pour into greased 9x13-inch pan.

TO MAKE SAUCE:

1. In another bowl, combine melted butter, brown sugar, cinnamon, flour, and water. Stir in nuts. Pour on top of cake batter. Marbleize with fork.
2. Bake 30 to 40 minutes. Do not overbake.

TO MAKE GLAZE:

1. In small bowl, blend powdered sugar, butter, vanilla, and milk.
2. Frost cake with glaze while cake is still warm.

Best-Yet Oatmeal Cake

Esther L. Miller - *Fredericktown, Ohio*

YIELDS

18 servings

CAKE INGREDIENTS:

1¾ cups boiling water

1 cup quick oats

½ cup butter

⅓ cup sugar

1 cup brown sugar

3 eggs

1¾ cups flour

1 teaspoon baking soda

1 teaspoon baking powder

½ teaspoon salt

1 teaspoon vanilla

TOPPING INGREDIENTS:

6 tablespoons butter

1 cup brown sugar

¼ cup milk

¾ cup shredded coconut

¾ cup chopped pecans

EQUIPMENT:

Mixing bowl with lid

Handheld mixer

Small bowl

9x13-inch pan

Saucepan

Spoon

TO MAKE CAKE:

1. Preheat oven to 350 degrees.

2. Put boiling water in bowl and add oats and butter. Cover and let stand 15 minutes.

3. Add sugar, brown sugar, and eggs, beating well.

4. In separate bowl, combine flour, baking soda, baking powder, and salt. Add to oat mixture. Add vanilla. Mix well.

5. Pour into greased 9x13-inch pan.

6. Bake 30 to 40 minutes.

7. When done, immediately spread with topping.

TO MAKE TOPPING:

1. In saucepan, mix topping ingredients and cook over low heat until bubbles appear.

2. Spread over baked cake.

3. Put under oven broiler at high heat for 2 minutes. Watch to make sure it doesn't get too dark.

PUMPKIN SHEET CAKE

CLARA MILLER - *Fredericktown, Ohio*

YIELDS

18 servings

CAKE INGREDIENTS:

1 (16 ounce) can pumpkin

2 cups sugar

1 cup vegetable oil

4 eggs, lightly beaten

2 cups flour

2 teaspoons baking soda

1 teaspoon cinnamon

½ teaspoon salt

FROSTING INGREDIENTS:

5 tablespoons butter or
   margarine, softened

3 ounces cream cheese,
   softened

1 teaspoon vanilla

1¾ cups powdered sugar

3 to 4 teaspoons milk

Chopped nuts

EQUIPMENT:

3 mixing bowls

Handheld mixer

10x15-inch jelly roll pan

Spatula

TO MAKE CAKE:

1. Preheat oven to 350 degrees.

2. In large bowl, use mixer to beat pumpkin, sugar, and oil. Add eggs and mix well.

3. In separate bowl, combine flour, baking soda, cinnamon, and salt. Add to pumpkin mixture and mix well. Pour into greased 10x15-inch jelly roll pan.

4. Bake 25 to 30 minutes or until cake tests done. Cool.

TO MAKE FROSTING:

1. In bowl, use mixer to beat butter, cream cheese, and vanilla until smooth. Gradually add powdered sugar, mixing well. Gradually add milk until frosting reaches desired spreading consistency.

2. Frost cake and sprinkle with nuts.

Never-Fail Red Velvet Cake

Jesse and Rose Raber - *Montgomery, Indiana*

YIELDS

24 servings

CAKE INGREDIENTS:

2¼ cups sugar

1⅛ cups shortening

3 eggs

3 tablespoons Nesquik chocolate drink mix

3 tablespoons red food coloring

3 tablespoons water

1½ cups buttermilk

3⅜ cups cake flour

¾ teaspoon salt

1½ teaspoons baking soda

1½ teaspoons vinegar

FROSTING INGREDIENTS:

1 cup milk

¼ cup flour

1 cup sugar

1 cup shortening

1 teaspoon vanilla

EQUIPMENT:

3 mixing bowls

Handheld mixer

Small bowl

Sifter

10x15-inch jelly roll pan

Spatula

Saucepan

TO MAKE CAKE:

1. Preheat oven to 350 degrees.

2. In bowl, use mixer to cream sugar, shortening, and eggs well.

3. In small bowl, drizzle Nesquik and food coloring into water. Add to creamed mixture. Add buttermilk.

4. Sift flour and salt 3 times. Add to first mixture.

5. Dissolve baking soda in vinegar. Add to creamed mixture. Spread in greased and floured 10x15-inch jelly roll pan.

6. Bake 15 to 17 minutes. Do not overbake.

TO MAKE FROSTING:

1. In saucepan, cook milk and flour until thick. Cool.

2. In bowl, cream sugar, shortening, and vanilla. Add flour mixture and beat well.

Rhubarb Upside-Down Cake

Gwyn Auker - *Elk Horn, Kentucky*

YIELDS
8 servings

CRUST INGREDIENTS:
¼ cup butter, softened
¾ cup brown sugar
3 cups diced rhubarb
2 tablespoons sugar

BATTER INGREDIENTS:
½ cup butter, softened
1 cup sugar
2 eggs, separated
1 teaspoon vanilla
1½ cups flour
2 teaspoons baking powder
½ teaspoon salt
½ cup milk
¼ teaspoon cream of tartar

EQUIPMENT:
2 small bowls
9-inch round cake pan
2 large mixing bowls
Handheld mixer
Spatula
Saucepan

TO MAKE CRUST:

1. Preheat oven to 325 degrees.

2. In small bowl, combine butter and brown sugar. Spread in greased 9-inch round cake pan.

3. Layer with rhubarb and sprinkle with sugar.

TO MAKE BATTER:

1. In mixing bowl, use mixer to cream butter and sugar. Beat in egg yolks and vanilla.

2. In separate bowl, combine flour, baking powder, and salt. Add to creamed mixture alternately with milk.

3. In small bowl, use clean mixer beaters to beat egg whites with cream of tartar until stiff peaks form. Fold into batter. Spoon batter over rhubarb.

4. Bake 40 to 45 minutes or until done.

5. Serve with whipped cream.

SHOOFLY CAKE

MARIE MARTIN - *Ephrata, Pennsylvania*

YIELDS

18 servings

INGREDIENTS:

1 cup light (mild) molasses
2¼ cups boiling water
1 tablespoon baking soda
¾ cup vegetable oil
4 cups flour
2⅓ cups (1 pound) brown sugar

EQUIPMENT:

2 mixing bowls
9x13-inch pan
Spoon

INSTRUCTIONS:

1. Preheat oven to 350 degrees.

2. In bowl, combine molasses, boiling water, and baking soda.

3. In separate bowl, mix oil, flour, and brown sugar until mixture forms crumbs. Reserve 1 cup crumbs for topping. Stir remaining crumbs into molasses mixture.

4. Pour batter into greased 9x13-inch pan. Top with reserved crumbs.

5. Bake 40 to 45 minutes.

SOUR CREAM SPICE CAKE

Mary Ann Yoder - *Woodhull, New York*

YIELDS
18 servings

BATTER INGREDIENTS:
½ cup shortening
2 cups brown sugar
3 eggs, separated
1 cup sour cream
1¾ cups flour
2 teaspoons cinnamon
1 teaspoon cloves
1 teaspoon allspice
½ teaspoon salt
1 teaspoon vanilla

ICING INGREDIENTS:
1 cup brown sugar
2 tablespoons butter
Pinch salt
3 tablespoons shortening
¼ cup milk
1½ cups powdered sugar
1 teaspoon vanilla

EQUIPMENT:
2 mixing bowls
Handheld mixer
Small bowl
9x13-inch pan
Spoon
Saucepan

TO MAKE BATTER:

1. Preheat oven to 350 degrees.

2. In bowl, use mixer to cream shortening and brown sugar. Beat in egg yolks and sour cream.

3. In separate bowl, combine flour, cinnamon, cloves, allspice, and salt. Add to creamed mixture and beat well. Add vanilla.

4. In small bowl, use clean mixer beaters to beat egg whites until stiff and fold into batter. Pour into greased 9x13-inch pan.

5. Bake 25 minutes. Cool.

TO MAKE ICING:

1. In saucepan, combine sugar, butter, salt, and shortening. Bring to a boil and add milk. Boil 3 minutes over medium-low heat. Cool.

2. Add powdered sugar and beat well. Stir in vanilla.

Texas Sheet Cake

Mrs. Leander Miller - *Cashton, Wisconsin*

YIELDS

18 servings

BATTER INGREDIENTS:

2 cups flour

2 cups sugar

1 cup margarine or butter, melted

3 tablespoons cocoa powder

1 cup water

2 eggs, beaten

½ cup sour milk

1 teaspoon baking soda

¼ teaspoon salt

1 teaspoon vanilla

FROSTING INGREDIENTS:

3 tablespoons cocoa powder

½ cup margarine or butter, melted

6 tablespoons milk

1 teaspoon vanilla

3½ cups (1 pound) powdered sugar

1 cup nuts, chopped

EQUIPMENT:

2 mixing bowls

Saucepan

9x13-inch pan

Spoon

Small bowl

TO MAKE BATTER:

1. Preheat oven to 350 degrees.

2. In large bowl, combine flour and sugar.

3. In saucepan, mix melted margarine and cocoa. Add water. Bring to a boil.

4. Pour over flour and sugar mixture. Add eggs, milk, baking soda, salt, and vanilla. Mix well. Pour into greased 9x13-inch pan.

5. Bake 25 minutes or until done. Cool.

TO MAKE FROSTING:

1. Place powdered sugar in mixing bowl.

2. In small bowl, stir cocoa into melted margarine. Add milk and vanilla. Pour over powdered sugar and mix well.

3. Frost cake and sprinkle with nuts.

WHITE-AS-SNOW CAKE

ADA MAST - *Kalona, Iowa*

YIELDS

9 servings

INGREDIENTS:

1½ cups flour
4½ teaspoons baking powder
1½ cups white sugar
1 teaspoon salt
½ cup shortening
1 cup milk, divided
4 egg whites
1 teaspoon vanilla

EQUIPMENT:

Mixing bowl
Sifter
Handheld mixer
9x9-inch pan
Spatula

INSTRUCTIONS:

1. Preheat oven to 350 degrees.

2. Sift dry ingredients into mixing bowl. Add shortening (softened but not melted) and ⅔ cup milk. Beat until batter is well blended and glossy. Add remaining milk, egg whites, and vanilla. Beat until smooth.

3. Bake in well-greased 9x9-inch pan 30 minutes.

4. Frost as desired.

Peaches-and-Cream Coffee Cake

Betty Miller - *Decatur, Indiana*

YIELDS

8 to 10 servings

BATTER INGREDIENTS:

⅔ cup flour

1 teaspoon baking powder

½ teaspoon salt

1 egg

½ cup milk

3 tablespoons melted butter

1 large can sliced peaches or 2½ cups sweetened fresh peaches

FILLING INGREDIENTS:

1 (8 ounce) package cream cheese, softened

½ cup sugar

3 tablespoons peach juice

TOPPING INGREDIENTS:

1 tablespoon sugar

½ teaspoon cinnamon

EQUIPMENT:

2 mixing bowls

Handheld mixer

8-inch round pan

2 small bowls

TO MAKE BATTER:

1. Preheat oven to 350 degrees.

2. In mixing bowl, mix flour, baking powder, and salt. Add egg, milk, and butter. Beat with mixer. Pour into well-greased 8-inch round pan.

3. Drain peaches, reserving juice in small bowl. Arrange peaches over batter.

4. Spoon filling over peaches.

5. Sprinkle on topping.

6. Bake 35 minutes.

TO MAKE FILLING:

In mixing bowl, use mixer to combine cream cheese, sugar, and peach juice.

TO MAKE TOPPING:

Blend sugar and cinnamon in small bowl. Sprinkle over filling.

Sour Cream Coffee Cake

Rachel D. Miller - *Millersburg, Ohio*

YIELDS
12 servings

CAKE INGREDIENTS:
½ cup butter
1 cup sugar
2 eggs
1 cup sour cream
1 teaspoon baking soda
1½ teaspoons vanilla
2 cups flour, divided
1 teaspoon baking powder
½ teaspoon salt

TOPPING INGREDIENTS:
½ cup flour
½ cup brown sugar
1 teaspoon cinnamon
3 tablespoons melted butter

FILLING INGREDIENTS:
2 egg whites
½ cup shortening
2 teaspoons vanilla
2 tablespoons marshmallow crème
2 cups powdered sugar

EQUIPMENT:
3 mixing bowls
Handheld mixer
3 small bowls
2 (9 inch) pie pans
Spoon
Spatula

TO MAKE CAKE:

1. Preheat oven to 350 degrees.
2. In mixing bowl, use mixer to cream butter and sugar well. Beat in eggs, one at a time.
3. In small bowl, combine sour cream with baking soda and vanilla.
4. In separate bowl, combine flour, baking powder, and salt.
5. To creamed mixture, add 1 cup flour mixture, then sour cream mixture, then remaining flour mixture. Pour batter into 2 greased foil pie pans.
6. Top with crumb topping.
7. Bake 25 minutes or until cakes spring back when centers are touched. Cool.
8. Remove cakes from pans and slice both cakes horizontally. Top three layers with cream filling and stack all layers.

TO MAKE TOPPING:

1. In small bowl, combine flour, brown sugar, cinnamon, and melted butter until crumbly.
2. Sprinkle topping over batter.

TO MAKE FILLING:

1. In mixing bowl, beat egg whites until frothy.
2. In another bowl, beat shortening until glossy. Add egg whites and mix well. Add vanilla and marshmallow crème. Slowly beat in powdered sugar.
3. Spread over three cake layers and stack.

WALNUT COFFEE CAKE

Fran Nissley - *Campbellsville, Kentucky*

YIELDS
18 servings

CAKE INGREDIENTS:
3 cups wheat flour
¾ cup honey
5 teaspoons baking powder
12 tablespoons butter
2 teaspoons cinnamon
1½ cups milk
2 eggs
1½ teaspoons salt
2 teaspoons vanilla

TOPPING INGREDIENTS:
½ cup honey
4 tablespoons butter
4 teaspoons cinnamon
1 cup chopped walnuts

EQUIPMENT:
Mixing bowl
Handheld mixer
9x13-inch cake pan
Knife

TO MAKE CAKE:
1. Preheat oven to 375 degrees.
2. Combine all ingredients in large bowl with mixer and pour into greased 9x13-inch pan.
3. Cover batter with topping and swirl in.
4. Bake 20 minutes.

TO MAKE TOPPING:
1. In bowl, mix all ingredients well and cover cake batter.
2. Swirl in topping with knife.

Happiness is like jam—you can't spread even a little without getting some of it on yourself.

Funny Cake

Miriam Brunstetter - *Easton, Pennsylvania*

YIELDS
8 servings

CAKE BATTER INGREDIENTS:
1¼ cups flour
¾ cup sugar
2 teaspoons baking powder
¼ cup shortening, softened
1 egg
½ cup milk
½ teaspoon vanilla

BASE INGREDIENTS:
1 (9 inch) unbaked pie shell
1 cup sugar
¼ cup cocoa powder
¾ cup hot water
1 teaspoon vanilla

EQUIPMENT:
2 mixing bowls
Handheld mixer
9-inch pie pan
Spatula

TO MAKE CAKE BATTER:

1. Preheat oven to 350 degrees.

2. In bowl, use mixer to combine all cake batter ingredients. Beat well and set aside.

TO MAKE BASE:

1. Fit pie dough to 9-inch pie pan.

2. In bowl, combine sugar, cocoa, water, and vanilla. Pour into unbaked pie shell.

3. Carefully pour cake batter on top.

4. Bake 45 minutes.

CARAMEL FROSTING

MARTHA PETERSHEIM - *Junction City, Ohio*

INGREDIENTS:

2 cups brown sugar
2 cups heavy cream
2 tablespoons butter
1 teaspoon vanilla

EQUIPMENT:

Saucepan
Spoon

INSTRUCTIONS:

1. In saucepan, bring brown sugar, cream, and butter to soft boil stage. Remove from heat and stir until light and fluffy. Add vanilla.

2. Spread on cake or cinnamon rolls.

FLUFFY COCOA FROSTING

MARTHA YODER - *Crofton, Kentucky*

INGREDIENTS:

¼ cup butter, softened
¼ cup heavy cream
1 teaspoon vanilla
⅛ cup cocoa powder
2 cups powdered sugar

EQUIPMENT:

Mixing bowl
Handheld mixer

INSTRUCTIONS:

In bowl, cream butter until light in color. Beat in cream and vanilla. Add cocoa. Slowly add powdered sugar until fluffy.

Coconut Pecan Frosting

Mrs. Harvey R. Miller - *South Dayton, New York*

INGREDIENTS:

1 cup evaporated milk or cream

1 cup sugar

3 egg yolks

2 tablespoons margarine or butter

1 teaspoon vanilla

1⅓ cups coconut

1 cup pecans, chopped

EQUIPMENT:

Saucepan

Spoon

INSTRUCTIONS:

1. In saucepan, cook milk, sugar, egg yolks, margarine, and vanilla over medium heat, stirring constantly, for 12 minutes or until thickened. Cool.

2. Add coconut and pecans. Beat until thick enough to spread.

Fluffy Cream Cheese Frosting

Jolene Bontrager - *Topeka, Indiana*

Great for topping cupcakes

INGREDIENTS:

4 ounces cream cheese, softened

1 (7 ounce) jar marshmallow crème

1 (8 ounce) tub nondairy whipped topping

EQUIPMENT:

Mixing bowl

Handheld mixer

Spatula

INSTRUCTIONS:

1. In bowl, beat cream cheese and marshmallow crème until well blended. Fold in whipped topping.

2. Keep refrigerated.

VARIATIONS:

- Lemon. Add 2 tablespoons lemon juice and 1 tablespoon lemon zest.

- Chocolate. Add 3 ounces semisweet chocolate, melted and slightly cooled.

- Coconut. Add ½ cup toasted coconut.

Peanut Butter Frosting

Anita Lorraine Petersheim - *Fredericktown, Ohio*

INGREDIENTS:

½ cup creamy peanut butter
5 to 6 tablespoons milk
1 teaspoon vanilla
2 cups powdered sugar

EQUIPMENT:

Mixing bowl
Handheld mixer
Spatula

INSTRUCTIONS:

In bowl, beat peanut butter and add milk and vanilla. Slowly add powdered sugar. Beat until fluffy.

The sign on the covered bridge reads:

11 FT 6 IN
CLEARANCE

WARNING
THE BRIDGE
IS UNSAFE
5 TONS

DESSERTS

Desserts are the ultimate comfort food.
Baked in one dish, these desserts are easy to put together.
Serve with whipped cream or ice cream to elevate
them to another level of goodness.

Apple Crisp

Fran Nissley - *Campbellsville, Kentucky*

YIELDS

12 servings

INGREDIENTS:

2 quarts apple pie filling
1 cup butter, melted
1 teaspoon salt
1 cup honey
¾ cup wheat bran
5 cups quick oats
3 cups wheat flour

EQUIPMENT:

Mixing bowl
Spoon
9x13-inch pan

INSTRUCTIONS:

1. Preheat oven to 350 degrees.

2. Put apple pie filling on bottom of 9x13-inch pan.

3. In bowl, mix butter, salt, and honey. Add bran, oats, and flour. Mix well and cover filling.

4. Bake 35 minutes until bubbly around the edges.

Apple Walnut Cobbler

Lois Rhodes - *Harrisonburg, Virginia*

YIELDS

9 servings

INGREDIENTS:

1¼ cups sugar, divided
½ teaspoon cinnamon
¾ cup coarsely chopped walnuts, divided
4 cups sliced tart apples
1 cup flour
1 teaspoon baking powder
¼ teaspoon salt
1 egg, beaten
½ cup evaporated milk
⅓ cup margarine, melted

EQUIPMENT:

Small bowl
Spoon
8x8-inch pan
2 mixing bowls
Sifter

INSTRUCTIONS:

1. Preheat oven to 325 degrees.
2. In small bowl, mix ½ cup sugar, cinnamon, and ½ cup nuts.
3. Place apples in bottom of greased 8-inch square baking dish. Sprinkle with cinnamon mixture.
4. In one mixing bowl, sift together remaining ¾ cup sugar, flour, baking powder, and salt.
5. In second bowl, combine egg, milk, and margarine. Add flour mixture and blend until smooth. Pour over apples. Sprinkle with remaining ¼ cup nuts.
6. Bake 50 minutes.
7. Serve with whipped topping or whipped cream sprinkled with cinnamon if desired.

BLACKBERRY PUDDING COBBLER

MRS. PAUL SCHROCK - *Marion, Michigan*

YIELDS

12 servings

INGREDIENTS:

⅓ cup butter

2 cups sugar, divided

2 cups flour

1 teaspoon salt

2 teaspoons baking powder

1 cup milk

2 cups fresh or frozen
   blackberries

2 cups boiling water

EQUIPMENT:

Mixing bowl

Spoon

9x13-inch pan

Small bowl

INSTRUCTIONS:

1. Preheat oven to 350 degrees.

2. In mixing bowl, cream butter and 1 cup sugar. Add flour, salt, baking powder, and milk to creamed mixture. Mix well and spread in greased 9x13-inch pan. Pour blackberries on top of batter.

3. In small bowl, combine remaining 1 cup sugar and 2 cups boiling water, and pour over berries. (May add more blackberries or liquid according to taste.)

4. Bake 50 minutes.

Note: Other fruit or berries may be substituted for the blackberries.

Magic Cobbler

Rosanna Helmuth - *Arthur, Illinois*

YIELDS
9 servings

INGREDIENTS:

½ cup butter

¾ cup milk

2 cups sugar, divided

1 cup flour

1½ teaspoons baking powder

2 cups fruit (peaches, apples, blueberries, blackberries, etc.)

EQUIPMENT:

8x11-inch pan

Mixing bowl

Spoon

INSTRUCTIONS:

1. Preheat oven to 350 degrees.

2. In 8x11-inch pan, melt butter in heating oven.

3. In mixing bowl, combine milk, 1 cup sugar, flour, and baking powder. Pour over melted butter but do not stir. Spread fruit on top and sprinkle with remaining 1 cup sugar. Again, do not stir.

4. Bake 30 to 40 minutes or until fruit is soft.

Peach Cobbler

Rhoda M. Schwartz - *Decatur, Indiana*

YIELDS

9 servings

INGREDIENTS:

1 cup flour
1 cup sugar
½ teaspoon salt
2 teaspoons baking powder
¾ cup milk
¼ cup margarine, melted
2½ to 3 cups sliced peaches

EQUIPMENT:

Mixing bowl
Spoon
8x8-inch baking dish

INSTRUCTIONS:

1. Preheat oven to 350 degrees.

2. In bowl, mix flour, sugar, salt, baking powder, and milk. Pour into baking dish and level. Pour margarine on top, but don't stir. Place peaches on top.

3. Bake 40 to 45 minutes.

BREAD PUDDING

EMMIE SCHWARTZ - *Berne, Indiana*

YIELDS

12 servings

PUDDING INGREDIENTS:

1 loaf homemade bread
2 cups heavy cream
2 cups milk
3 large eggs, beaten
2 cups sugar
1 teaspoon vanilla
1½ teaspoons cinnamon
¼ cup butter, melted

SAUCE INGREDIENTS:

½ cup butter
1 cup sugar
⅔ cup heavy cream

EQUIPMENT:

Large mixing bowl
Spoons
9x13-inch pan
Saucepan

TO MAKE PUDDING:

1. Preheat oven to 325 degrees.

2. Tear bread into small pieces and place in large bowl. Add cream and milk. Let stand 10 minutes.

3. Stir mixture well. Add eggs, sugar, vanilla, and cinnamon. Stir well.

4. Pour butter into 9x13-inch pan. Spoon pudding mixture into pan.

5. Bake uncovered 55 to 60 minutes.

TO MAKE SAUCE:

1. In saucepan, cook butter, sugar, and cream until sugar dissolves. Simmer 5 minutes.

2. Drizzle over pudding.

SWEDISH APPLE PUDDING

THELMA ZOOK - *Oakland, Maryland*

YIELDS

12 servings

PUDDING INGREDIENTS:

1½ cups sugar

2 eggs

2 cups flour

2 teaspoons cinnamon

⅔ cup shortening

6 apples, chopped

2 teaspoons baking soda

1 teaspoon nutmeg

¼ teaspoon salt

SAUCE INGREDIENTS:

1½ cups brown sugar

2 tablespoons flour

1 cup water

2 tablespoons butter

1 teaspoon vanilla or
   maple flavoring

EQUIPMENT:

Large mixing bowl

Spoons

9x13-inch pan

Saucepan

TO MAKE PUDDING:

1. Preheat oven to 350 degrees.

2. Add ingredients to bowl in order given. Mix well. Pour into greased 9x13-inch pan.

3. Bake 1 hour.

TO MAKE SAUCE:

1. In saucepan, cook all ingredients until thick.

2. Cool and pour over cake.

Cinnamon Pudding

Anna Stutzman - *Arcola, Illinois*

YIELDS
12 servings

INGREDIENTS:
4 tablespoons margarine
4 cups brown sugar
4 cups water
2 cups flour
2 cups sugar
4 tablespoons margarine
4 teaspoons baking powder
4 teaspoons cinnamon
4 teaspoons vanilla
2¼ cups milk
¾ cup chopped nuts
Whipped topping or
   ice cream (optional)

EQUIPMENT:
Saucepan
Spoon
Mixing bowl
9x13-inch pan

INSTRUCTIONS:
1. Preheat oven to 350 degrees.
2. In saucepan, combine 4 tablespoons margarine, brown sugar, and water. Bring to a boil.
3. Meanwhile, in bowl, combine flour, sugar, 4 tablespoons margarine, baking powder, cinnamon, vanilla, and milk. Mix well. Spread in greased 9x13-inch pan and pour boiling sugar mixture over top.
4. Bake 10 minutes.
5. Sprinkle with nuts and bake 10 minutes longer.
6. Serve warm with whipped topping or ice cream if desired.

Date Pudding

Lovina Nissley - *Chatham, Virginia*

YIELDS
9 servings

PUDDING INGREDIENTS:
1 cup brown sugar
1 cup flour
1 teaspoon butter
½ cup milk
¼ teaspoon salt
1 tablespoon baking soda
1 cup dates
½ cup chopped nuts
Whipped topping

SYRUP INGREDIENTS:
1½ cups water
1 cup brown sugar
1 tablespoon butter
1 tablespoon vanilla

EQUIPMENT:
Mixing bowl
Spoon
9x9-inch baking dish

TO MAKE PUDDING:

1. Preheat oven to 350 degrees.

2. In bowl, mix brown sugar, flour, butter, milk, salt, baking soda, and dates. Pour into baking dish. Sprinkle with nuts.

TO MAKE SYRUP:

1. In saucepan, boil water and melt brown sugar and butter. Add vanilla. Pour syrup over batter.

2. Bake 30 to 35 minutes.

3. Serve with whipped topping.

MAGIC MOCHA PUDDING

MRS. GID MILLER - *Norwalk, Wisconsin*

YIELDS

8 to 9 servings

BATTER INGREDIENTS:

1 cup sugar

2 teaspoons instant coffee granules

6 tablespoons butter

1 cup milk

Vanilla to taste

1 egg

1½ cups flour

2½ teaspoons baking powder

½ teaspoon salt

SAUCE INGREDIENTS:

1 cup sugar

2 tablespoons cocoa powder

1½ tablespoons cornstarch

2½ cups water

EQUIPMENT:

Mixing bowl

Spoons

8x8-inch pan

Saucepan

TO MAKE BATTER:

1. Preheat oven to 350 degrees.

2. Combine sugar, coffee, butter, milk, and vanilla. Mix well. Beat in egg. Add flour, baking powder, and salt. Pour into baking dish.

TO MAKE SAUCE:

1. Combine sugar, cocoa, cornstarch, and water in saucepan, and boil until thickened.

2. Pour half the chocolate sauce over batter.

3. Bake 30 to 35 minutes.

4. Add remaining sauce before serving. Serve hot with milk or cold with whipped cream.

How sweet are thy words unto my taste! yea, sweeter than honey to my mouth!

PSALM 119:103

SPICY GINGERBREAD WITH CREAMY CARAMEL SAUCE

RUTH MULLET - *Cass City, Michigan*

YIELDS

9 to 12 servings

GINGERBREAD INGREDIENTS:

½ cup sugar
3 tablespoons butter
1 egg
1 teaspoon ginger
1 teaspoon cinnamon
1 teaspoon baking soda
1 cup molasses
½ cup milk or hot water
1½ cups flour

SAUCE INGREDIENTS:

1 cup brown sugar
2 tablespoons butter
½ cup light corn syrup
½ cup heavy cream
½ teaspoon vanilla

EQUIPMENT:

Mixing bowl
Spoons
9x9-inch pan
Saucepan

TO MAKE GINGERBREAD:

1. Preheat oven to 350 degrees.

2. In large bowl, combine ingredients in order given. Pour into 9x9-inch pan.

3. Bake 40 minutes. Serve with creamy caramel sauce.

TO MAKE SAUCE:

1. In saucepan, combine brown sugar, butter, and corn syrup. Heat to full boil, stirring constantly.

2. Remove from heat and add cream and vanilla.

OLD-FASHIONED APPLE DUMPLINGS

SUSAN BYLER - *Crab Orchard, Kentucky*

YIELDS

6 servings

DUMPLING INGREDIENTS:

6 medium apples

2 cups flour

2½ teaspoons baking powder

½ teaspoon salt

⅔ cup shortening

½ cup milk

Cinnamon

Sugar

SAUCE INGREDIENTS:

2 cups water

2 cups brown sugar

¼ teaspoon cinnamon

¼ cup butter

EQUIPMENT:

Paring knife

Mixing bowl

Fork or pastry cutter

Rolling pin

Small bowl

Spoons

Saucepan

9x13-inch pan

TO MAKE DUMPLINGS:

1. Preheat oven to 375 degrees.

2. Cut apples in half, pare, and core.

3. To make pastry, combine flour, baking powder, and salt in bowl. Cut in shortening until crumbly. Sprinkle milk over mixture and press lightly, just enough to hold together.

4. Roll dough as for pastry and cut into 6 squares. Place apple half on each square.

5. In small bowl, mix 1 part cinnamon with 2 parts sugar.

6. Fill cavities of apples with cinnamon and sugar mixture. Top with other halves of apples. Fold and pat dough up around apples to cover completely. Fasten edges on top by pinching together. Moisten fingers if necessary. Place dumplings 1 inch apart in greased 9x13-inch baking pan.

TO MAKE SAUCE:

1. In saucepan, cook water, brown sugar, and cinnamon for 5 minutes. Remove from heat and add butter. Pour over dumplings.

2. Bake 35 to 40 minutes.

3. Serve hot with rich milk or cream.

Brown Sugar Dumplings

Lydiann Yoder - *Andover, Ohio*

YIELDS

12 servings

INGREDIENTS:

1 cup brown sugar
2 cups hot water
2 tablespoons butter
½ cup nuts or raisins
½ cup sugar
1 cup flour
2 teaspoons baking powder
1 teaspoon vanilla
½ cup water or milk

EQUIPMENT:

Saucepan
Spoon
Mixing bowl
9x13-inch pan

INSTRUCTIONS:

1. Preheat oven to 350 degrees.

2. In saucepan, mix brown sugar, hot water, and butter. Bring to a boil. Stir in nuts.

3. In bowl, mix sugar, flour, and baking powder until crumbly. Add vanilla and water, stirring until smooth.

4. Pour hot syrup into 9x13-inch pan. Drop batter by spoonfuls onto syrup.

5. Bake 30 to 40 minutes.

6. Before serving, break into small pieces. Serve with ice cream or whipped cream.

Tiny Chocolate Cherry Cheesecakes

Rachel D. Miller - *Millersburg, Ohio*

YIELDS
24 cheesecakes

INGREDIENTS:

1 cup flour
¼ cup sucanat
¼ cup cocoa powder
½ cup cold butter
2 tablespoons water
1 (8 ounce) package cream cheese, softened
1 egg
¼ cup honey
1 teaspoon vanilla
Cherry jam or pie filling

EQUIPMENT:

2 mixing bowls
Spoons
Fork
Mini cupcake pans—24 wells
Handheld mixer

INSTRUCTIONS:

1. Preheat oven to 325 degrees.

2. In bowl, combine flour, sucanat, and cocoa. Cut in butter. Add water. Toss with fork until dough forms ball. Shape into 24 balls.

3. Press dough into bottom and sides of well-greased mini cupcake pans.

4. In mixing bowl, use mixer to beat cream cheese, egg, honey, and vanilla until smooth.

5. Into each dough cup, spoon 1 tablespoon filling.

6. Bake 15 to 18 minutes. Cool 30 minutes before removing from pans.

7. Put about 2 teaspoons jam or pie filling on top of each.

WHITE CHOCOLATE RASPBERRY CHEESECAKE

ESTHER MAST - *Gambier, Ohio*

Plan ahead and make this excellent treat the day before serving.

YIELDS
12 servings

INGREDIENTS:
1½ cups graham cracker crumbs
1 cup sugar, divided
⅓ cup butter, melted
3 (8 ounce) packages cream cheese, softened
⅓ cup sour cream
3 tablespoons flour
1 teaspoon vanilla
3 eggs, lightly beaten
1 (10 ounce) package white or vanilla baking chips
¼ cup raspberry pie filling

EQUIPMENT:
2 mixing bowls
9-inch springform pan
Mixing bowl
Spoon
Handheld mixer
Knife

INSTRUCTIONS:

1. Preheat oven to 325 degrees.

2. In small bowl, combine cracker crumbs, ¼ cup sugar, and butter. Press into bottom of greased 9-inch pan.

3. In large bowl, use mixer to beat cream cheese with ¾ cup sugar until smooth. Beat in sour cream, flour, and vanilla. Add eggs. Beat on slow speed just until combined. Fold in baking chips. Pour batter over crust.

4. Drop pie filling by teaspoonfuls over batter. Cut through batter with knife to swirl in filling.

5. Bake 80 to 85 minutes.

6. Carefully run knife around edges to loosen from pan. Cool 1 hour. Refrigerate overnight.

RHUBARB TORTE

MRS. BRUCE TROYER - *Crab Orchard, Kentucky*

CRUST INGREDIENTS:

1½ cups flour
2 tablespoons sugar
Pinch salt
½ cup butter

FILLING INGREDIENTS:

2¼ cups chopped rhubarb
1½ cups sugar
2 to 3 cups whole milk
2 to 4 tablespoons flour
3 egg yolks
1 teaspoon vanilla

TOPPING INGREDIENTS:

3 egg whites
¼ teaspoon cream of tartar
6 tablespoons sugar

EQUIPMENT:

2 mixing bowls
Spoons
8x10-inch baking pan
Saucepan

CRUST INSTRUCTIONS:

1. Preheat oven to 325 degrees.
2. In bowl, mix crust ingredients until crumbly and press into 8x10-inch baking pan.
3. Bake 20 to 25 minutes.

FILLING INSTRUCTIONS:

1. Combine filling ingredients in saucepan and cook, stirring, until thick.
2. Pour over cooled crust.

TOPPING INSTRUCTIONS:

1. In mixing bowl, beat egg whites until foamy. Add cream of tartar and sugar. Beat until stiff. Spread over filling.
2. Brown in oven 10 to 15 minutes.

PIES

The Amish have a reputation for making delectable pies, and pies are often the highlight of the dessert menu at an Amish restaurant. Making a pie doesn't have to be intimidating. With a little practice working with piecrust, anyone can do it.

IMPOSSIBLE-TO-RUIN PIE

RACHEL YODER - *Fultonville, New York*

No piecrust needed!

YIELDS

6 to 8 servings

INGREDIENTS:

4 eggs

2 cups milk

1 tablespoon vanilla

½ cup sweetener (sugar, honey, maple syrup)

½ cup flour

½ teaspoon salt

1 cup coconut

EQUIPMENT:

Mixing bowl

Handheld mixer

9-inch glass pie pan

INSTRUCTIONS:

1. Preheat oven to 350 degrees.

2. In bowl, beat eggs until light in color. Add milk, vanilla, and sweetener, mixing well. Add flour, salt, and coconut, mixing well. Pour into 9-inch glass pie pan.

3. Bake 45 minutes, just until set.

AMISH SAWDUST PIE

MARIE D. HERSHBERGER - *Laurelville, Ohio*

YIELDS

6 to 8 servings

INGREDIENTS:

9-inch unbaked pie shell

1⅔ cups coconut

1½ cups graham cracker crumbs

1½ cups chopped nuts

1½ cups sugar

1 cup egg whites

EQUIPMENT:

9-inch pie pan

Mixing bowl

Spoon

INSTRUCTIONS:

1. Preheat oven to 350 degrees.

2. Form pastry to fit bottom and sides of pie pan. Trim, fold, and pinch edges.

3. Combine coconut, cracker crumbs, nuts, and sugar. Mix in egg whites (do not beat). Pour mixture into pie shell.

4. Bake 35 to 40 minutes

Coconut Oatmeal Pie

Mrs. John Miller - *Navarre, Ohio*

YIELDS
6 to 8 servings

INGREDIENTS:
9-inch unbaked pie shell
1 cup light corn syrup
½ cup brown sugar
⅓ cup butter, melted
1 teaspoon vanilla
⅛ teaspoon salt
3 eggs, beaten
½ cup flaked coconut
½ cup quick oats

EQUIPMENT:
9-inch pie pan
Mixing bowl
Spoon

INSTRUCTIONS:
1. Preheat oven to 350 degrees.
2. Form pastry to fit bottom and sides of pie pan. Trim, fold, and pinch edges.
3. In mixing bowl, combine all ingredients in order given and mix well. Pour into unbaked pie shell.
4. Bake 30 to 35 minutes or until pie tests done.

COUNTRY FAIR PIE

SUSAN SCHWARTZ - *Berne, Indiana*

YIELDS

6 to 8 servings

INGREDIENTS:

9-inch unbaked pie shell

½ cup butter or margarine, melted

1 cup sugar

½ cup flour

2 eggs

1 teaspoon vanilla

1 cup (6 ounces) semisweet chocolate chips

½ cup butterscotch chips

1 cup chopped nuts

EQUIPMENT:

9-inch pie pan

Mixing bowl

Spoon

INSTRUCTIONS:

1. Preheat oven to 325 degrees.

2. Form pastry to fit bottom and sides of pie pan. Trim, fold, and pinch edges.

3. In bowl, beat butter, sugar, flour, eggs, and vanilla until well blended. Stir in chips and nuts. Pour into unbaked pie shell.

4. Bake 1 hour or until golden brown. Cool on wire rack.

FUNERAL PIE

ESTHER STAUFFER - *Port Trevorton, Pennsylvania*

YIELDS

6 to 8 servings

INGREDIENTS:

1 cup raisins

2 cups hot water

8-inch unbaked pie shell and pastry strips for lattice top

1¼ cups sugar

4 tablespoons flour

1 egg, well beaten

Zest and juice of 1 lemon

¼ teaspoon salt

1 tablespoon butter

EQUIPMENT:

Small bowl

8-inch pie pan

Double boiler

Spoon

INSTRUCTIONS:

1. Wash raisins and soak in bowl of hot water 1 hour or longer. Drain.

2. Form pastry to fit bottom and sides of pie pan. Leave untrimmed.

3. In double boiler, combine raisins, sugar, flour, egg, lemon zest and juice, salt, and butter. Mix thoroughly and cook until thickened. Cool.

4. Pour into pie shell and weave pastry strips over filling to make lattice top. Seal and crimp edges.

5. Bake in preheated 450-degree oven 10 minutes. Reduce heat to 350 degrees and continue baking until nicely browned (about 30 minutes).

SHOOFLY PIE

MATTIE HERSHBERGER - *Heuvelton, New York*

YIELDS

4 pies (6 to 8 servings each)

CRUMB TOPPING INGREDIENTS:

4 cups flour

2 cups sugar

3 tablespoons butter

3 tablespoons lard or shortening

1 teaspoon cinnamon

¾ teaspoon nutmeg

¾ teaspoon ginger

Pinch salt

FILLING INGREDIENTS:

4 (9 inch) unbaked pie shells

2 cups cane molasses

2 cups warm water

1 tablespoon baking soda

EQUIPMENT:

4 (9 inch) pie pans

2 mixing bowls

Fork

Spoon

TO MAKE TOPPING:

1. In bowl, use fork to blend all ingredients until mixture forms crumbs.

2. Note: Butter and lard (or shortening) tablespoon measurements should be level. Crumbs will be dry.

TO MAKE FILLING:

1. Preheat oven to 350 degrees.

2. Form pastry to fit bottom and sides of pie pans. Trim, fold, and pinch edges.

3. In bowl, combine molasses, water, and baking soda. Divide mixture equally into 4 unbaked pie shells.

4. Divide crumbs and sprinkle evenly on top of filling in pie shells. Let stand 10 minutes.

5. Bake 30 to 40 minutes or until done.

LEMON SHOOFLY PIE

Mrs. Henry Leid - *Elkton, Kentucky*

*This recipe won a first-place ribbon at
the Malheur County Fair in Ontario, Oregon.*

YIELDS

6 to 8 servings

**FILLING
INGREDIENTS:**

9-inch unbaked pie shell
1 egg
Zest of 2 lemons
Juice of 2 lemons, strained
2 tablespoons flour
½ cup sugar
½ cup molasses
¾ cup boiling water

**CRUMB TOPPING
INGREDIENTS:**

1½ cups flour
½ cup sugar
½ cup shortening or butter,
   softened
½ teaspoon baking soda

EQUIPMENT:

9-inch pie pan
2 mixing bowls
Spoon
Fork

TO MAKE FILLING:

1. Preheat oven to 350 degrees.

2. Form pastry to fit bottom and sides of pie pan. Trim, fold, and pinch edges.

3. In bowl, combine egg, lemon zest, lemon juice, flour, sugar, and molasses. Slowly incorporate boiling water. Pour into unbaked pie shell.

TO MAKE CRUMB TOPPING:

1. In bowl, blend flour, sugar, shortening, and baking soda with fork until mixture forms crumbs. Sprinkle crumbs evenly on top of filling.

2. Bake 45 to 60 minutes.

Pilgrim Pie

MRS. DAVID J. KURTZ - *Smicksburg, Pennsylvania*

YIELDS

6 to 8 servings

INGREDIENTS:

9-inch unbaked pie shell

2 eggs

¾ cup sugar

¼ cup butter, melted

½ cup corn syrup

½ cup water

½ teaspoon maple or vanilla flavoring

½ teaspoon salt

½ cup quick oats

½ cup nuts and/or chocolate chips

EQUIPMENT:

9-inch pie pan

Mixing bowl

Handheld mixer

INSTRUCTIONS:

1. Preheat oven to 350 degrees.

2. Form pastry to fit bottom and sides of pie pan. Trim, fold, and pinch edges.

3. In bowl, beat eggs until thick and light yellow, about 3 minutes. Beat in sugar, butter, corn syrup, water, flavoring, and salt. Stir in oats and chocolate chips. Pour filling into pie shell.

4. Bake 50 to 60 minutes. Cool completely before serving.

PECAN PIE

EDNA IRENE MILLER - *Arthur, Illinois*

YIELDS

6 to 8 servings

INGREDIENTS:

9-inch unbaked pie shell
3 eggs
1½ cups maple syrup
2 tablespoons butter, melted
2 tablespoons spelt flour
1 teaspoon vanilla
¼ teaspoon salt
1 cup pecans

EQUIPMENT:

9-inch pie pan
Mixing bowl
Handheld mixer
Spoon

INSTRUCTIONS:

1. Preheat oven to 350 degrees.

2. Form pastry to fit bottom and sides of pie pan. Trim, fold, and pinch edges.

3. In mixing bowl, beat eggs. Add maple syrup, butter, flour, vanilla, and salt. Stir in pecans. Pour into pie shell.

4. Bake 30 minutes or until set and browned.

PERFECT PUMPKIN PIE

MRS. HARVEY R. MILLER - *South Dayton, New York*

YIELDS

6 to 8 servings

INGREDIENTS:

2 (9 inch) unbaked pie shells
1 cup pumpkin or squash, cooked
1½ cups brown sugar
1 teaspoon salt
½ teaspoon allspice
½ teaspoon cloves
1 teaspoon cinnamon
4 tablespoons flour
4 eggs, separated
4 cups milk
1 teaspoon vanilla

EQUIPMENT:

2 (9 inch) pie pans
Mixing bowl
Spoon
Handheld mixer
Knife

INSTRUCTIONS:

1. Preheat oven to 375 degrees.

2. Form pastry to fit bottom and sides of pie pans. Trim, fold, and pinch edges.

3. In bowl, combine all ingredients except egg whites until well blended.

4. In separate bowl, beat egg whites with clean beaters until stiff. Fold into pumpkin mixture. Pour into unbaked pie shells.

5. Bake 1 hour or until knife inserted in pie comes out clean.

SOUR CREAM PUMPKIN PIES

EDNA MILLER - *Apple Creek, Ohio*

YIELDS

2 pies (6 to 8 servings each)

FILLING INGREDIENTS:

2 (9 inch) unbaked pie shells

1 (15 ounce) can pumpkin

1 (14 ounce) can sweetened condensed milk

2 teaspoons pumpkin pie spice

½ teaspoon ginger (optional)

½ teaspoon nutmeg (optional)

2 eggs, beaten

½ teaspoon salt

½ cup nuts, minced (optional)

CREAM TOPPING INGREDIENTS:

1 (8 ounce) package cream cheese, softened

¾ cup sugar

1½ cups sour cream

CRUMB TOPPING INGREDIENTS:

1 cup brown sugar

1 cup flour

6 tablespoons butter, softened

Chopped nuts (optional)

EQUIPMENT:

2 (9 inch) pie pans

2 mixing bowls

Spoon

Handheld mixer

Small bowl

Fork

TO MAKE FILLING:

1. Preheat oven to 425 degrees.

2. Form pastry to fit bottom and sides of pie pans. Trim, fold, and pinch edges.

3. In mixing bowl, combine pumpkin, milk, spices, eggs, and salt. Divide into pie shells and bake 15 minutes. Reduce heat to 350 degrees and bake 20 minutes longer.

TO MAKE CREAM TOPPING:

1. Meanwhile, in bowl, use mixer to blend cream cheese and sugar. Mix in sour cream until smooth.

2. Divide mixture in half and spread evenly on hot pies.

TO MAKE CRUMB TOPPING:

1. In small bowl, combine brown sugar, flour, and butter with fork to make crumbly mixture.

2. Divide crumbs to cover both pies. Garnish with nuts if desired. Bake at 350 degrees another 15 minutes.

SWEET POTATO PIE

SHARRI NOBLETT - *Memphis, Texas*

YIELDS

6 to 8 servings

INGREDIENTS:

9-inch unbaked pie shell

2 cups cooked mashed sweet potatoes

1 (14 ounce) can condensed sweetened milk

2 large eggs

1 tablespoon vanilla

¼ teaspoon salt

EQUIPMENT:

9-inch pie pan

Mixing bowl

Handheld mixer

INSTRUCTIONS:

1. Preheat oven to 350 degrees.

2. Form pastry to fit bottom and sides of pie pan. Trim, fold, and pinch edges.

3. In bowl, combine sweet potatoes, milk, eggs, vanilla, and salt. Beat until smooth. Pour into pie shell.

4. Bake 60 minutes.

Strawberry Rhubarb Pie

Mrs. Ray Hershberger - *Scottville, Michigan*

YIELDS

6 to 8 servings

INGREDIENTS:

9-inch unbaked pie shell and top

3 cups chopped rhubarb

1 cup fresh strawberries, sliced

2 eggs

1½ cups sugar

3 tablespoons flour

Dash salt

EQUIPMENT:

9-inch pie pan

2 mixing bowls

Handheld mixer

INSTRUCTIONS:

1. Preheat oven to 350 degrees.

2. Form pastry to fit bottom and sides of pie pan. Trim, fold, and pinch edges.

3. In bowl, mix rhubarb and strawberries. Put into pie shell.

4. In another bowl, beat eggs, sugar, flour, and salt. Pour over fruit.

5. Top with crust. Crimp edges to close. Cut vent.

6. Bake 1 hour until browned and bubbly.

STREUSEL-TOP FRUIT PIE

ESTHER BORNTRAGER - *Beeville, Texas*

YIELDS

6 to 8 servings

PASTRY CRUST INGREDIENTS:

2 teaspoons sugar

1 teaspoon salt

½ cup vegetable oil

2 tablespoons milk

1½ cups flour

FRUIT FILLING INGREDIENTS:

½ cup powdered sugar

⅓ cup flour

4 cups sliced fresh peaches or 2 (29 ounce) cans sliced peaches, drained*

STREUSEL TOPPING INGREDIENTS:

¾ cup flour

½ cup brown sugar

½ teaspoon cinnamon

⅓ cup butter or margarine, softened

EQUIPMENT:

3 mixing bowls

Spoons

9-inch pie pan

TO MAKE PASTRY CRUST:

1. In mixing bowl, combine sugar, salt, oil, and milk. Add flour to form soft pastry dough.

2. Press pastry into bottom and up sides of 9-inch pie pan. Flute edges if desired.

TO MAKE FILLING:

1. Combine powdered sugar and flour in mixing bowl. Toss in peaches, stirring to coat well.

2. Spoon into unbaked pastry crust.

TO MAKE STREUSEL TOPPING:

1. In bowl, combine flour, brown sugar, cinnamon, and butter to form crumb mixture. Spoon over peaches.

2. Bake pie in preheated 375-degree oven 40 to 45 minutes until topping is golden brown.

Note: Four cups fresh blueberries or fresh halved strawberries may be substituted for peaches.

ANGEL CREAM PIE

BETTY MILLER - *Goshen, Indiana*

YIELDS

6 to 8 servings

INGREDIENTS:

9-inch unbaked pie shell

2 egg whites, stiffly beaten

1 cup half-and-half

1 cup heavy whipping cream

½ cup sugar

⅛ teaspoon salt

2 tablespoons (slightly rounded) flour

1 teaspoon vanilla

EQUIPMENT:

9-inch pie pan

Mixing bowl

Handheld mixer

Saucepan

Whisk

Spatula

INSTRUCTIONS:

1. Preheat oven to 350 degrees.

2. Form pastry to fit bottom and sides of pie pan. Trim, fold, and pinch edges.

3. In bowl, beat egg whites until stiff.

4. In saucepan, combine half-and-half and whipping cream. Warm only slightly. Turn off heat and add sugar, salt, and flour, beating in with whisk. Add vanilla and fold in stiffly beaten egg whites. Pour into unbaked pie shell.

5. Bake 45 minutes or until slightly jiggly.

LEMON BLOSSOM PIE

IDA R. SCHWARTZ - *Salem, Indiana*

YIELD

3 pies (6 to 8 servings each)

FILLING INGREDIENTS:

3 cups water
½ teaspoon salt
6 egg yolks, beaten
2 cups sugar
½ cup cornstarch
4 tablespoons butter, melted
½ cup lemon juice
3 (9 inch) baked pie shells

MERINGUE INGREDIENTS:

6 egg whites
½ cup sugar

EQUIPMENT:

Saucepan
2 mixing bowls
Handheld mixer
Spatula
3 (9 inch) pie pans

TO MAKE FILLING:

1. In saucepan, bring water and salt to a boil.
2. In bowl, mix egg yolks, sugar, cornstarch, butter, and lemon juice until smooth. Slowly add to boiling water. Cook until thick.
3. Pour hot filling into baked pie shells.

TO MAKE MERINGUE:

1. Preheat oven to 350 degrees.
2. In bowl, use clean beaters to beat egg whites until stiff peaks form. Add sugar and beat well. Spread equally over pies.
3. Bake until meringue is golden brown, approximately 10 to 15 minutes.

VARIATIONS:

- ¾ teaspoon lemon flavoring may be added to filling
- ½ teaspoon cream of tartar may be added to meringue

Vanilla Crumb Pie

Mrs. Samuel J. Schwartz - *Bryant, Indiana*

YIELDS

3 pies (6 to 8 servings each)

FILLING INGREDIENTS:

3 (9 inch) unbaked pie shells
1 cup brown sugar
1 cup corn syrup
2 cups water
2 tablespoons flour
1 egg
½ teaspoon cream of tartar
1 teaspoon vanilla
1 teaspoon baking soda

CRUMB TOPPING INGREDIENTS:

2 cups pastry flour
1 cup brown sugar
½ cup lard
½ teaspoon baking soda
1 teaspoon cream of tartar

EQUIPMENT:

3 (9 inch) pie pans
Saucepan
Spoon
2 mixing bowls
Handheld mixer
Fork

TO MAKE FILLING:

1. Preheat oven to 350 degrees.
2. Form pastry to fit bottom and sides of pie pan. Trim, fold, and pinch edges.
3. In saucepan, boil brown sugar, corn syrup, water, and flour for 1 minute. Set aside.
4. In large bowl, beat egg, cream of tartar, vanilla, and baking soda. Add to syrup. Divide mixture equally between 3 pie shells.

TO MAKE CRUMB TOPPING:

1. In bowl, combine flour, brown sugar, lard, baking soda, and cream of tartar with fork until crumbly.
2. Divide crumb mixture over top of each pie.
3. Bake 45 minutes.

Chocolate Brownie Pie

Lovina M. Schwartz - *Geneva, Indiana*

YIELDS

6 to 8 servings

INGREDIENTS:

9-inch unbaked pie shell

2 squares unsweetened chocolate

2 tablespoons butter

3 large eggs

½ cup sugar

¾ cup dark corn syrup

¾ cup pecans

EQUIPMENT:

9-inch pie pan

Double boiler or microwaveable bowl

Mixing bowl

Handheld mixer

Spoon

INSTRUCTIONS:

1. Preheat oven to 375 degrees.

2. Form pastry to fit bottom and sides of pie pan. Trim, fold, and pinch edges.

3. In double boiler or microwaveable bowl, melt chocolate and butter.

4. In mixing bowl, use mixer to blend eggs, sugar, and corn syrup. Beat thoroughly. Add chocolate mixture and beat again. Stir in nuts. Pour into pie shell.

5. Bake 40 to 50 minutes.

Easy Piecrust

Mary Yoder - *Goshen, Indiana*

YIELDS

10-inch piecrust. A doubled recipe will fill 3 (9 inch) pans.

INGREDIENTS:

1½ cups flour
½ teaspoon salt
½ scant cup vegetable oil
2 tablespoons sugar
2 tablespoons milk
¼ teaspoon baking powder

EQUIPMENT:

Mixing bowl
Fork
10-inch pie pan

INSTRUCTIONS:

Combine all ingredients with fork. Press into pie pan and up sides. Crimp the edges.

TO MAKE PIE:

1. If baking with filling, bake 10 minutes at 400 degrees then 25 minutes longer at 350 degrees.

2. If baking empty piecrust, prick bottom and sides several times with fork to keep crust from bubbling. Bake 10 to 15 minutes at 400 degrees.

PIECRUST

MRS. ANDY A. HERSHBERGER - *Navarre, Ohio*

YIELDS
enough to fill (9 inch) pie pan

INGREDIENTS:
1 cup butter
½ cup buttermilk
1 egg
1 cup spelt flour

EQUIPMENT:
Mixing bowl
Fork or pastry cutter
Rolling pin
(9 inch) pie pan

INSTRUCTIONS:

1. In bowl, mix butter, buttermilk, and egg with fork. Cut in flour until right consistency to roll out crust. Don't overmix.

2. Divide into balls, cover tightly, and chill.

3. Roll out dough to desired thickness.

4. Form pastry to fit bottom and sides of pie pan. Trim, fold, and pinch edges.

Piecrust

For the flakiest possible piecrust, use ice-cold water. Add a pinch of salt for better taste.

Chocolate Piecrust

Mary Miller - *Junction City, Ohio*

YIELDS
enough to fill 9-inch pie pan

INGREDIENTS:
1¼ cups flour
½ teaspoon salt
⅓ cup sugar
¼ cup cocoa powder
½ cup shortening
½ teaspoon vanilla
2 to 3 tablespoons cold water

EQUIPMENT:
Mixing bowl
Sifter
Fork or pastry cutter
Rolling pin
9-inch pie pan

INSTRUCTIONS:

In mixing bowl, sift together flour, salt, sugar, and cocoa. Cut in shortening. Add vanilla. Sprinkle with cold water. Form into ball. Roll out and place in pie pan.

NOTES FOR USE:

- Piecrust can be baked empty and filled when cool with instant vanilla pudding.

- Or fill unbaked piecrust with something like pecan pie filling, butterscotch filling, or custard, and bake.

- Also bake pastry trimmings to crumble for topping.

PASTRIES

Pastries are bakery confectionaries that delight by their complex looks, taste, and texture. A sought-after Amish pastry is their doughnuts, often found freshly made at farmers' markets and flea markets.

HANS WASCHTLIN

MRS. SAMUEL LEE - *Plymouth, Illinois*

A great treat for children!

YIELD WILL VARY.

INGREDIENTS:
Leftover pie dough trimmings
Jelly

EQUIPMENT:
Rolling pin
Knife
Pie pan

INSTRUCTIONS:

1. Preheat oven to 350 degrees.
2. Roll out dough until thin. Spread with jelly.
3. Roll up like jelly roll and cut in ½-inch slices. Lay slices on pie pan cut side down.
4. Bake 15 to 20 minutes.

Cream Cheese Flitzers

Katurah Miller - *Loudonville, Ohio*

Easy and wonderful for a quick tea party or coffee break. Delicious!

YIELDS
approximately 24 servings

INGREDIENTS:
1 (8 ounce) package cream
  cheese
¼ cup sugar
1 egg yolk
1 cup sugar
Butter
1 teaspoon cinnamon
1 loaf sandwich bread

EQUIPMENT:
Mixing bowl
Handheld mixer
Small saucepan
Small shallow bowl
Spoon
Knife
Rolling pin
Baking sheet

INSTRUCTIONS:
1. Preheat oven to 350 degrees.
2. In mixing bowl, combine cream cheese, ¼ cup sugar, and egg yolk until fluffy.
3. In small saucepan, melt butter.
4. In small shallow bowl, combine 1 cup sugar and cinnamon.
5. Trim crust from bread. Roll slices thin with rolling pin. Spread each slice with cream cheese mixture. Roll up. Dip in butter then in sugar mixture. Set on baking sheet.
6. Bake 15 minutes.

The secret of success is to start from scratch and then keep on scratching.

Fruit Pizza

Leona Mullet - *Burton, Ohio*

YIELDS

16 to 20 servings

CRUST INGREDIENTS:

½ cup butter

¾ cup sugar

1 egg

1½ cups flour

1 teaspoon baking powder

¼ teaspoon salt

FRUIT LAYER INGREDIENTS:

1 (8 ounce) package cream cheese

½ cup sugar

1 (8 ounce) tub nondairy whipped topping

Dash of vanilla

Any fruits of your choice, cut or whole

GLAZE INGREDIENTS:

1¾ cups white sugar

¼ teaspoon salt

1 package Kool-Aid (any flavor)

4 cups water

¾ cup Clear Jel

½ cup water

EQUIPMENT:

2 mixing bowls

Spoons

14-inch round pizza pan or 10x15-inch jelly roll pan

Handheld mixer

2 small bowls

Medium saucepan

TO MAKE CRUST:

1. Preheat oven to 350 degrees.

2. In mixing bowl, cream butter, sugar, and egg. Add flour, baking powder, and salt. Mix well. Pat dough evenly onto ungreased pan.

3. Bake on pan 12 minutes. Remove from oven. Cool completely.

TO MAKE FRUIT LAYER:

1. In bowl, use mixer to blend cream cheese and sugar. Mix in whipped topping and dash of vanilla. Spread on crust.

2. Layer on fruits of your choice, cut or whole.

TO MAKE GLAZE:

1. In small bowl, mix sugar, salt, and Kool-Aid.

2. Place 4 cups water in saucepan and add sugar mixture. Stir well as it comes to a boil.

3. In small bowl, mix Clear Jel with ½ cup water. Add to boiling sauce, stirring constantly until thickened. Cool completely.

4. Spread over top of fruit pizza. Chill.

Baked Doughnuts

Mrs. Reuben (Martha) Byler - *Atlantic, Pennsylvania*

YIELDS

approximately 24 doughnuts

DOUGH INGREDIENTS:

1 tablespoon yeast

3 tablespoons sugar

2 cups warm water

3 cups store-bought doughnut mix

2 cups flour

FILLING INGREDIENTS:

2 (3 ounce) boxes instant vanilla pudding

3 cups milk

1 (8 ounce) package cream cheese, softened

EQUIPMENT:

Large mixing bowl

Spoon

Jar ring or round biscuit cutter

Baking sheet

Knife

2 medium mixing bowls

Handheld mixer

TO MAKE DOUGH:

1. In large bowl, mix yeast and sugar. Add water and stir well. Add doughnut mix and flour. Mix well. Cover and let rise.

2. Roll out dough to ½-inch thick. Cut with jar ring or other round cutter. Let doughnuts rise on baking sheet.

3. Preheat oven to 350 degrees.

4. Bake 20 minutes or until golden brown. Cool.

5. Cut doughnuts in half. Spread with filling sandwich style.

TO MAKE FILLING:

1. In mixing bowl, mix pudding and milk.

2. In another bowl, beat cream cheese until smooth. Beat in pudding a little at a time.

NOTES:

- Doughnuts may be glazed.
- Add whipped topping to filling if it is too dense for your taste.
- Doughnuts are also good with fruit filling and vanilla frosting.

Cream-Filled Doughnut Bars

Lorene Herschberger - *Sullivan, Illinois*

These are delicious! When we get together for our family night, the girls often bring one pan of these. So good!

YIELDS
24 servings

DOUGHNUT BAR INGREDIENTS:
1 cup lukewarm water

1 tablespoon yeast

¼ cup brown sugar

1 egg, beaten

¼ cup vegetable oil

1 teaspoon salt

1 cup doughnut mix

3 cups flour

FILLING INGREDIENTS:
1 cup scalded milk

1 (3 ounce) box instant vanilla pudding mix

1 (8 ounce) package cream cheese

1 (8 ounce) tub nondairy whipped topping

EQUIPMENT:
2 mixing bowls

Spoons

10x15-inch jelly roll pan

Small rolling pin

Handheld mixer

Spatula

TO MAKE DOUGHNUT BARS:

1. In mixing bowl, combine water and yeast. Let stand until foamy. Mix in brown sugar, egg, oil, and salt. Add doughnut mix, mixing well. Add flour 1 cup at a time, kneading thoroughly. Cover and let rise 1 hour.

2. Punch down dough and roll out on large well-greased baking sheet. Let rise 1 hour.

3. Preheat oven to 350 degrees.

4. Bake 12 to 15 minutes.

5. Cool completely. Cut dough in half lengthwise.

TO MAKE FILLING:

1. In mixing bowl, use mixer to blend milk, pudding mix, and cream cheese. Add whipped topping and blend until smooth.

2. Spread filling on bottom layer of dough. Put other half of dough on top.

3. Frost with your favorite caramel frosting and sprinkle with cinnamon and sugar.

Best-Ever Cinnamon Rolls

VERENA N. SCHWARTZ - *Scottsburg, Indiana*

YIELDS
18 rolls

INGREDIENTS:
6 cups flour
1 cup sugar
4 teaspoons salt
3 tablespoons yeast
1 cup lard
4 eggs
3 cups lukewarm milk
4 cups flour
2 cups brown sugar
4 teaspoons cinnamon
¼ cup melted butter
Heavy cream

EQUIPMENT:
2 mixing bowls
Spoon
Rolling pin
Small bowl
Knife
9x13-inch pan

INSTRUCTIONS:

1. In large mixing bowl, combine 6 cups flour, sugar, salt, and yeast. Add lard, eggs, and milk, mixing well until smooth and elastic. Gradually add 4 cups flour and knead until smooth. (Do not grease bowl as you might for bread.) Let dough rise, punch it down, and let rise again.

2. Roll out dough into rectangle.

3. In small bowl, combine brown sugar, cinnamon, and butter. Spread over dough. Roll up dough from a long side and cut into ¾-inch slices. Put slices into greased 9x13-inch pan. Spoon 1 tablespoon of cream on each roll. Let rise.

4. Preheat oven to 350 degrees.

5. Bake 20 minutes.

6. Frost. I use cream cheese icing.

VARIATION:

To make fruit-filled rolls, omit cinnamon-sugar-butter mixture. Roll and slice the dough. Spoon on the cream, then add a spoonful of pie filling of your choice (we like raspberry) to the center of each roll. Bake.

Cinnamon Love Knots

Katie Schmidt - *Carlisle, Kentucky*

YIELDS

3 dozen rolls

INGREDIENTS:

2 tablespoons yeast
½ cup warm water
½ cup warm milk
½ cup butter, softened
½ cup sugar
2 eggs, beaten
4½ to 5 cups flour
2 cups sugar
2 tablespoons cinnamon
¾ cup butter, melted

EQUIPMENT:

2 mixing bowls
Spoon
Dish towel
Small bowl
Baking sheet

INSTRUCTIONS:

1. In mixing bowl, dissolve yeast in warm water. Let stand 5 minutes.

2. Add milk, ½ cup butter, ½ cup sugar, and eggs. Stir in enough flour for stiff dough. Turn onto floured surface. Knead until smooth and elastic. Place in greased bowl. Cover and let rise until doubled, about 1 to 1½ hours.

3. Punch down dough. Divide into 3 balls. Shape each ball into 12 balls, then roll each small ball into 8-inch ropes.

4. In small bowl, combine 2 cups sugar with cinnamon.

5. Dip each rope in melted butter, then coat in cinnamon-sugar mixture. Tie ropes into knots and place on baking sheet. Let knots rise.

6. Bake 12 to 14 minutes in preheated 375-degree oven.

The LORD is my portion, saith my soul; therefore will I hope in him.

LAMENTATIONS 3:24

Maple Twist Rolls
Verna Slabaugh - *Spickard, Missouri*

YIELDS

16 rolls

DOUGH INGREDIENTS:

¾ cup milk

¼ cup butter

1 tablespoon yeast dissolved in ¼ cup warm water

3 tablespoons white sugar

1 egg

½ teaspoon salt

1 teaspoon maple flavoring

2¼ to 3 cups flour

FILLING INGREDIENTS:

¼ cup butter, softened

½ cup brown sugar

½ cup nuts

1 teaspoon cinnamon

1 teaspoon maple flavoring

FROSTING INGREDIENTS:

1 cup powdered sugar

1 tablespoon butter, softened

½ teaspoon maple flavoring

1 to 2 tablespoons milk

EQUIPMENT:

2 mixing bowls

Spoons

Small bowl

Rolling pin

Baking sheet

TO MAKE DOUGH:

1. Preheat oven to 400 degrees.

2. In large bowl, combine milk, butter, yeast dissolved in water, sugar, egg, salt, and maple flavoring. Add flour and combine well. Divide dough into 3 equal balls and roll out into equal-sized rectangles (roughly 6x16 inches).

TO MAKE FILLING:

1. In small bowl, combine all ingredients.

2. Spread half of filling on first layer of dough, cover with next layer of dough, spread other half of filling on it. Put last layer of dough on top. Cut into 1-inch strips and twist each strip once. Place on baking sheet and let rise.

3. Bake 12 to 15 minutes.

TO MAKE FROSTING:

In mixing bowl, blend powdered sugar, butter, maple flavoring, and enough milk to reach the right consistency. Drizzle over top of slightly cooled baked rolls.

OVERNIGHT ROLLS

BETTY MILLER - *Decatur, Indiana*

YIELDS

18 rolls

INGREDIENTS:

1 cup boiling water
½ cup sugar
½ cup butter
½ teaspoon salt
½ teaspoon sugar
2 tablespoons warm water
1 package yeast
2 eggs, beaten
4 cups flour, divided
Melted butter
Brown sugar
Cinnamon

EQUIPMENT:

Mixing bowl
2 small bowls
Spoons
Rolling pin
Pastry brush
Knife
9x13-inch pan

INSTRUCTIONS:

1. In large bowl, mix boiling water, ½ cup sugar, butter, and salt. Cool to lukewarm.

2. In small bowl, mix ½ teaspoon sugar, warm water, and yeast, stirring to dissolve. Add to first mixture. Add eggs. Stir in 2 cups flour. Beat 3 minutes. Add remaining flour and beat until smooth.

3. Refrigerate dough until cold.

4. Roll out dough to ½-inch-thick rectangle. Brush with melted butter.

5. In small bowl, combine brown sugar and cinnamon and sprinkle over dough.

6. Roll up dough and slice to make 18 rolls. Place slices in greased 9x13-inch pan.

7. Chill in refrigerator overnight.

8. In morning, bake 15 minutes in preheated 375-degree oven.

9. Glaze if desired.

Raspberry Cream Rolls

David L. Byler - *New Wilmington, Pennsylvania*

YIELDS

18 servings

DOUGH INGREDIENTS:

1 cup milk at 70 to 80 degrees

¼ cup water

1 tablespoon sugar

1 tablespoon yeast

¼ cup butter, softened

1 egg

1 teaspoon salt

¼ cup instant vanilla pudding mix

4 cups bread flour, divided

FILLING INGREDIENTS:

1 egg

⅓ cup sugar

1 (8 ounce) package cream cheese, softened

1 (16 ounce) can raspberry pie filling

ICING INGREDIENTS:

4 ounces cream cheese, softened

1½ cups powdered sugar

½ teaspoon vanilla

¼ cup butter

1½ teaspoons milk

EQUIPMENT:

Small bowl

3 mixing bowls

Spoons

Rolling pin

Knife

9x13-inch pan

Handheld mixer

TO MAKE DOUGH:

1. In small bowl, blend milk, water, sugar, and yeast. Set aside.

2. In mixing bowl, mix butter, egg, salt, and pudding mix. Mix in first mixture. Gradually add 2 cups flour at a time.

3. Roll out half of dough. Slice and cut into small pieces. Put pieces into greased 9x13-inch pan, covering bottom.

TO MAKE FILLING:

1. In bowl, mix egg, sugar, and cream cheese. Spread over dough. Spread pie filling over cream cheese mixture.

2. Roll out remaining half of dough, slice, and cut into pieces. Place dough on top of filling. Cover and let rise 1 hour.

3. Uncover and bake in preheated 350-degree oven 25 minutes or until done. Let rolls cool before icing.

TO MAKE ICING:

1. In mixing bowl, use mixer to blend all ingredients until smooth.

2. Spread over rolls. Cut into squares.

Sour Cream Rolls

Menno and Esther Yoder - *Berlin, Pennsylvania*

YIELDS

2 dozen rolls

DOUGH INGREDIENTS:

1 tablespoon yeast

¼ cup warm water

¼ cup sugar

2 eggs

½ teaspoon salt

½ cup sour cream

¼ cup butter, melted

2¾ to 3 cups flour

FILLING INGREDIENTS:

Melted butter

½ cup sugar

½ cup brown sugar

½ teaspoon cinnamon

GLAZE INGREDIENTS:

¾ cup sugar

1 tablespoon milk

1 tablespoon vanilla

¼ cup butter, melted

½ cup sour cream

Chopped nuts

EQUIPMENT:

Mixing bowls

Spoons

Dish towel

Rolling pin

Pastry brush

2 small bowls

9x13-inch pan

Handheld mixer

TO MAKE DOUGH:

1. In large bowl, soften yeast in warm water. Add sugar, eggs, salt, sour cream, and butter. Gradually add flour to form soft dough. Cover and let rise until doubled.

2. Knead dough on floured surface. Roll out dough in 2 (12 inch) circles.

TO MAKE FILLING:

1. Brush dough circles with melted butter.

2. In small bowl, combine sugar, brown sugar, and cinnamon. Sprinkle over butter.

3. Cut each circle into 12 pie-shaped wedges. Roll up dough, starting at wide end. Place in greased 9x13-inch pan. Let rise.

4. Bake 20 minutes in preheated 350-degree oven.

TO MAKE GLAZE:

1. In small bowl, combine sugar, milk, vanilla, butter, and sour cream.

2. Pour over warm rolls. Sprinkle with nuts.

Pumpkin Rolls

Elizabeth Borntrager - *Brown City, Michigan*

YIELDS
8 to 10 slices

CAKE INGREDIENTS:
3 eggs
1 cup sugar
⅔ cup pumpkin
1 teaspoon lemon juice
¾ cup flour
1 teaspoon baking powder
2 teaspoons cinnamon
1 teaspoon ginger
½ teaspoon nutmeg
½ teaspoon salt
Powdered sugar

FILLING INGREDIENTS:
1 cup powdered sugar
¼ cup butter, softened
6 ounces cream cheese
1 teaspoon vanilla

EQUIPMENT:
3 mixing bowls
Handheld mixer
Spoons
Parchment paper (optional)
10x15-inch jelly roll pan
Dish towel

TO MAKE CAKE:

1. Preheat oven to 375 degrees.

2. In mixing bowl, beat eggs on high speed 5 minutes. Beat in sugar. Stir in pumpkin and lemon juice.

3. In separate bowl, combine flour, baking powder, cinnamon, ginger, nutmeg, and salt. Fold into pumpkin mixture. Spread in greased and floured 10x15-inch jelly roll pan (or line pan with parchment paper).

4. Bake 15 minutes.

5. Remove cake from oven and turn onto clean linen towel dusted with powdered sugar. Roll towel and cake together. Cool.

TO MAKE FILLING:

1. Use mixer to blend powdered sugar, butter, cream cheese, and vanilla until smooth.

2. Unroll cooled cake, spread with filling, and roll back up. Chill.

STRAWBERRY CREAM CAKE ROLL

LIZZIE SCHROCK - *Sullivan, Ohio*

YIELDS

10 slices

CAKE INGREDIENTS:

4 eggs
1 teaspoon vanilla extract
¾ cup sugar
¾ cup sifted cake flour
1 teaspoon baking powder
¼ teaspoon salt
Powdered sugar

FILLING INGREDIENTS:

1 cup heavy whipping cream
¼ cup sugar
½ teaspoon vanilla extract
2 cups frozen or fresh
   strawberries, cut up

EQUIPMENT:

3 mixing bowls
Handheld mixer
Spoons
Wax or parchment paper
10x15-inch jelly roll pan
Dish towel

TO MAKE CAKE:

1. Preheat oven to 375 degrees.

2. In mixing bowl, beat eggs and vanilla on high speed 5 minutes or until lemon colored. Gradually add sugar, beating until dissolved.

3. In separate bowl, combine flour, baking powder, and salt. Fold gently into egg mixture until just combined. Pour into jelly roll pan lined with wax paper. Spread batter evenly over pan.

4. Bake 10 to 12 minutes or until light brown.

5. Turn out onto dish towel sprinkled well with powdered sugar. Peel off paper from cake. Roll up towel and cake. Let cool.

TO MAKE FILLING:

1. In bowl, whip cream, sugar, and vanilla until fluffy.

2. Unroll cake and spread filling over it. Sprinkle with strawberries. Roll up cake again and chill 2 hours before serving.

3. Sprinkle with powdered sugar. Cut 1-inch slices. Garnish with additional strawberries and whipped cream if desired.

White Caramel Swiss Roll Cake

Jolene Bontrager - *Topeka, Indiana*

YIELDS

8 to 10 slices

CAKE INGREDIENTS:

1¾ cups flour

⅔ cup sugar

1 (3 ounce) box instant vanilla pudding mix

2 teaspoons baking powder

½ teaspoon salt

2 eggs

1¼ cups milk

½ cup vegetable oil

1 teaspoon vanilla

Powdered sugar

FILLING INGREDIENTS:

1 (8 ounce) package cream cheese, softened

⅔ cup brown sugar

⅛ teaspoon salt

1 teaspoon vanilla

1 (8 ounce) tub nondairy whipped topping

FROSTING INGREDIENTS:

½ cup butter, softened

1 cup brown sugar

1 cup sour cream

EQUIPMENT:

2 mixing bowls

Spoons

Handheld mixer

Parchment paper (optional)

10x15-inch jelly roll pan

Dish towel

Saucepan

TO MAKE CAKE:

1. Preheat oven to 350 degrees.

2. In mixing bowl, combine flour, sugar, pudding mix, baking powder, and salt. Add eggs, milk, oil, and vanilla. Blend well with mixer. Pour into well-greased and floured 10x15-inch jelly roll pan (or line pan with parchment paper).

3. Bake 15 to 20 minutes. Cool slightly. Turn out onto clean dish towel dusted with powdered sugar. Roll cake, starting from short side. Cool completely.

TO MAKE FILLING:

1. In bowl, use mixer to beat cream cheese, brown sugar, salt, and vanilla until light and fluffy. Fold in whipped topping.

2. Unroll cake and spread with filling. Reroll cake. Chill.

TO MAKE FROSTING:

1. In saucepan, bring butter and brown sugar to a boil for 2 minutes. Cool 30 minutes.

2. Stir in sour cream.

3. Cool completely in refrigerator before spreading over cake roll.

Note: For a shortcut, use a white cake mix for the cake portion.

CROISSANT ROLLS

KATHRYN TROYER - *Rutherford, Tennessee*

YIELDS

1½ to 2 dozen rolls

INGREDIENTS:

1 cup butter

⅓ cup flour

1½ cups warm water

1 tablespoon yeast

1 teaspoon salt

3 tablespoons brown sugar

2½ tablespoons potato flakes

⅓ cup dry milk

⅓ cup cornstarch

3 cups flour

1 egg

1 tablespoon milk

Sugar

EQUIPMENT:

4 mixing bowls

Pastry cutter

Wax paper

Rolling pin

Spoons

Towel

Small bowl

Pastry brush

2 baking sheets

INSTRUCTIONS:

1. In bowl, cut butter into ⅓ cup flour. Place on wax paper. Fold over paper and press or roll into 10x4-inch rectangle. Chill 1 hour, no longer.

2. Meanwhile, in large bowl, stir together warm water and yeast. Let sit to dissolve.

3. Stir salt, brown sugar, potato flakes, dry milk, cornstarch, and 3 cups flour into yeast mixture. Form soft dough. Knead lightly. Place in oiled bowl. Cover and let rise 1 hour.

4. On floured surface, roll yeast dough into 12-inch square. Place chilled butter mixture on center of square. Fold sides over chilled mixture. Roll into 12-inch square. Repeat the fold and roll 3 more times. Place in covered bowl and chill 1 hour.

5. Divide dough in half. Roll each half into 12-inch circle. Cut each circle into 8 to 12 wedges. Roll up wedges from widest edge to point. Place on greased baking sheets. Let rise 1 hour.

6. Preheat oven to 375 degrees.

7. In small bowl, mix egg and milk. Brush tops of rolls and sprinkle with sugar.

8. Bake 15 to 20 minutes until golden brown.

QUICK BREADS, BISCUITS, AND MUFFINS

Bread seems like a long task of rising and kneading and more rising. But not with these quick batters that result in both savory and sweet breads often associated with breakfast time.

APPLESAUCE SPICE PUFFS

IRENE MILLER - *Shipshewana, Indiana*

YIELDS
around 12 puffs

MUFFIN INGREDIENTS:

2 cups dry baking mix
⅓ cup sugar
1 teaspoon cinnamon
¼ teaspoon cloves
¼ teaspoon nutmeg
½ cup applesauce
¼ cup milk
1 egg, beaten
2 tablespoons vegetable oil

TOPPING INGREDIENTS:

½ cup butter
1 teaspoon cinnamon
½ cup sugar

EQUIPMENT:

Mixing bowl
Sifter
Spoons
Muffin tins
Small saucepan
Small bowl
Pastry brush

INSTRUCTIONS:

1. Preheat oven to 400 degrees.

2. Sift baking mix into large bowl. Stir in sugar, cinnamon, clove, and nutmeg. Add applesauce, milk, egg, and oil.

3. Fill greased muffin tins two-thirds full.

4. Bake 12 minutes.

TOPPING INSTRUCTIONS:

1. In small saucepan, melt butter.

2. In small bowl, combine cinnamon and sugar.

3. Brush muffin tops with melted butter and dip in cinnamon sugar mixture.

4. Serve warm.

Bacon 'n' Cheese Muffins

Ada Miller - *Norwalk, Wisconsin*

YIELDS

1 dozen muffins

INGREDIENTS:

½ pound bacon
Vegetable oil
1 egg, beaten
¾ cup milk
1¾ cups flour
¼ cup sugar
1 tablespoon baking powder
½ cup cornflakes
1 cup shredded cheese

EQUIPMENT:

Frying pan
2 medium bowls
Spoon
Muffin tin(s)—12 wells

INSTRUCTIONS:

1. Preheat oven to 400 degrees.

2. Fry bacon and reserve drippings. If necessary, add oil to drippings to make ¼ cup.

3. In medium bowl, combine drippings, egg, and milk. Set aside.

4. In separate bowl, combine flour, sugar, and baking powder. Add to drippings mixture and stir until moistened. Fold in crumbled bacon, cornflakes, and shredded cheese. Spoon into greased muffin tins.

5. Bake 15 to 20 minutes.

BEST BLUEBERRY MUFFINS

DAVID L. BYLER - *New Wilmington, Pennsylvania*

YIELDS
1 dozen muffins

INGREDIENTS:
1 cup oats
1 cup orange juice
3 cups flour
1 cup sugar
2½ teaspoons baking powder
1 teaspoon salt
½ teaspoon baking soda
1 cup vegetable oil
2 eggs
2 cups fresh or frozen
  blueberries
Sugar and cinnamon topping
  as desired

EQUIPMENT:
Mixing bowl
Spoon
Muffin tin(s)—12 wells

INSTRUCTIONS:
1. Preheat oven to 400 degrees.
2. In bowl, combine oats and orange juice. Add flour, sugar, baking powder, salt, baking soda, oil, and eggs, mixing well. Stir in blueberries. Fill greased muffin cups two-thirds full. Sprinkle well with cinnamon-sugar mixture.
3. Bake 18 to 22 minutes.

Baking Tip

For the best possible outcome, start out with your eggs and butter at room temperature. Ingredients will blend easier and faster.

Doughnut Muffins

Dorcas Marie Yoder - *Meyersdale, Pennsylvania*

YIELDS

1 dozen muffins

MUFFIN INGREDIENTS:

3 cups flour
1 cup sugar
1 cup brown sugar
2 teaspoons baking powder
1 teaspoon baking soda
½ teaspoon salt
1½ teaspoons cinnamon
½ teaspoon nutmeg
2 eggs
1½ cups apple cider
1 teaspoon vanilla

TOPPING INGREDIENTS:

¾ cup butter, melted
1½ cups sugar
3½ teaspoons cinnamon

EQUIPMENT:

Mixing bowl
2 small bowls
Spoon
Muffin tin(s)—12 wells
Pastry brush

MUFFIN INSTRUCTIONS:

1. Preheat oven to 350 degrees.

2. In mixing bowl, combine flour, sugar, brown sugar, baking powder, baking soda, salt, cinnamon, and nutmeg.

3. In small bowl, blend eggs, apple cider, and vanilla. Add to dry mixture until just moistened. Fill greased muffin cups two-thirds full.

4. Bake 20 to 25 minutes.

TOPPING INSTRUCTIONS:

1. Coat each warm muffin with butter.

2. In small shallow bowl, combine sugar and cinnamon. Roll buttered muffins in mixture.

Morning Glory Muffins

Dorothy Glick - *Augusta, West Virginia*

YIELDS

2½ dozen muffins

INGREDIENTS:

4 eggs
1⅓ cups vegetable oil
1 teaspoon vanilla
3 cups flour
1¼ cups brown sugar
3 teaspoons baking soda
¾ teaspoon salt
3 teaspoons cinnamon
3 cups shredded carrots
¾ cup flaked coconut
1 large apple, shredded
⅓ cup nuts
½ cup raisins

EQUIPMENT:

2 mixing bowls
Spoon
Muffin pans—30 wells

INSTRUCTIONS:

1. Preheat oven to 350 degrees.

2. In mixing bowl, beat eggs, oil, and vanilla.

3. In separate bowl, combine flour, brown sugar, baking soda, salt, and cinnamon. Stir into egg mixture just until moistened. Fold in nuts, raisins, carrots, coconut, and apple until just moistened. Spoon into greased muffin tins.

4. Bake 15 to 20 minutes.

COUNTRY PUMPKIN MUFFINS

AMANDA KUEPFER - *Chesley, Ontario, Canada*

YIELDS
2 dozen muffins

INGREDIENTS:
2 cups sugar
½ cup vegetable oil
2 eggs
2 cups pumpkin puree
3 cups flour
½ teaspoon baking powder
1 teaspoon baking soda
½ teaspoon ground cloves
¾ teaspoon cinnamon
½ teaspoon nutmeg
1 teaspoon salt
1½ cups raisins
1 cup chopped walnuts

EQUIPMENT:
2 mixing bowls
Spoon
Muffin pans—24 wells

INSTRUCTIONS:

1. Preheat oven to 375 degrees.

2. In mixing bowl, blend sugar, oil, eggs, and pumpkin. In separate bowl, combine flour, baking powder, baking soda, cloves, cinnamon, nutmeg, and salt. Add dry mix to pumpkin mixture. Fold in raisins and nuts. Spoon into well-greased or lined muffin tins.

3. Bake 15 minutes.

AMISH FRIENDSHIP STARTER

FROM *AMISH COOKING CLASS COOKBOOK*

This is a ten-day process.

TOTAL INGREDIENTS TO BE DIVIDED AND ADDED OVER SEVERAL DAYS:

¼ cup warm water

1 (¼ ounce) packet yeast

1½ cups plus 1 tablespoon sugar

3 cups milk

3 cups flour

EQUIPMENT:

Mixing bowl

Wooden spoon

Tea towel for covering

INSTRUCTIONS:

Day 1:

Put warm water in bowl and add yeast. Sprinkle 1 tablespoon sugar over it and let stand in warm place (about 10 minutes). Mix ½ cup sugar, 1 cup milk, 1 cup flour, and yeast mixture. Stir with wooden spoon. Do not use metal spoon as it will retard the yeast's growth. Cover loosely and let stand at room temperature overnight.

Days 2–4:

Stir starter each day with wooden spoon. Cover loosely again.

Day 5:

Stir in ½ cup sugar, 1 cup milk, and 1 cup flour. Mix well. Cover loosely.

Days 6–9:

Stir well each day and cover loosely.

Day 10:

1. Stir in ½ cup sugar, 1 cup milk, and 1 cup flour. The starter is now ready to use to make bread.

2. Remove 1 cup to make your first bread. Give 1 cup each to 2 friends, along with recipe for starter and your favorite Amish friendship bread. Store remaining starter in container in refrigerator (or freeze) to make future bread.

Amish Friendship Bread

FROM *AMISH COOKING CLASS COOKBOOK*

YIELDS

2 loaves

INGREDIENTS:

1 cup starter (see page 144)
3 eggs
1 cup vegetable oil
½ cup milk
½ teaspoon vanilla
2 cups flour
1 cup sugar
2 teaspoons cinnamon
1½ teaspoons baking powder
½ teaspoon salt
½ teaspoon baking soda
1 to 2 (3 ounce) boxes instant pudding (any flavor)
1 cup nuts, chopped (optional)
1 cup raisins (optional)
½ cup sugar
½ teaspoon cinnamon

EQUIPMENT:

2 (5x9-inch) loaf pans
2 mixing bowls
Small bowl
Spoons
Toothpick

INSTRUCTIONS:

1. Preheat oven to 325 degrees.

2. Grease and flour 2 large loaf pans.

3. In mixing bowl, mix starter, eggs, oil, milk, and vanilla.

4. In separate bowl, mix flour, 1 cup sugar, 2 teaspoons cinnamon, baking powder, salt, baking soda, pudding mix, and nuts and/or raisins, if desired. Add to liquid mixture and stir thoroughly.

5. In small bowl, mix ½ cup sugar and ½ teaspoon cinnamon, and dust greased pans lightly.

6. Pour batter evenly into pans and sprinkle remaining cinnamon-sugar mixture on top.

7. Bake 1 hour or until toothpick inserted in center of bread comes out clean.

OPTIONS:

- Use 2 (3 ounce) boxes pudding mix. Change flavor of pudding mix.

- Add up to 2 cups dried fruit or baking chips (Note: heavier add-ins may sink to bottom).

- Decrease fat by substituting ½ cup vegetable oil and ½ cup applesauce for 1 cup vegetable oil in recipe.

- Decrease eggs by using 2 eggs and ¼ cup mashed banana.

- Use large bundt pan rather than 2 loaf pans.

Apple Bread

Velma Schrock - *Goshen, Indiana*

This bread is a great gift to give along with a jar of homemade apple butter.

YIELDS
2 loaves

INGREDIENTS:
3 cups flour
2 teaspoons cinnamon
½ teaspoon baking powder
½ teaspoon salt
2 cups sugar
1 teaspoon baking soda
1 cup oil
4 large eggs
½ teaspoon vanilla
2 cups finely chopped apples
1 cup chopped nuts

EQUIPMENT:
2 mixing bowls
Spoon
2 (4x8-inch) bread pans
Parchment paper
Toothpick

INSTRUCTIONS:
1. Preheat oven to 350 degrees.
2. Combine flour, cinnamon, baking powder, salt, sugar, and baking soda.
3. In mixing bowl, blend oil, eggs, and vanilla. Add flour mixture, stirring just until moistened. Batter will be thick. Fold in apples and nuts.
4. Line 2 bread pans with parchment paper and grease or spray with oil. Divide batter into pans equally.
5. Bake 50 to 55 minutes, until toothpick inserted in middle comes out clean.
6. Cool in pan 10 minutes before removing.

Note: This bread can be wrapped in foil, placed in a plastic bag, and frozen.

Chocolate Chunk Banana Bread

Janine Merdian - *Lacon, Illinois*

YIELDS

1 loaf

INGREDIENTS:

1 cup mashed bananas

2 eggs, slightly beaten

⅓ cup vegetable oil

¼ cup milk

2 cups flour

1 cup sugar

2 teaspoons baking powder

¼ teaspoon salt

1 (4 ounce) bar Baker's German Sweet Baking Chocolate, coarsely chopped

½ cup chopped nuts

EQUIPMENT:

Mixing bowl

5x9-inch loaf pan

Spoon

Toothpick

INSTRUCTIONS:

1. Preheat oven to 350 degrees.

2. In mixing bowl, stir bananas, eggs, oil, and milk until well blended. Add flour, sugar, baking powder, and salt. Stir until moistened. Stir in chocolate and nuts.

3. Pour into greased loaf pan.

4. Bake 55 minutes or until toothpick in center comes out clean.

5. Cool in pan 10 minutes. Remove bread from pan and cool completely on wire rack.

Help my words to be gracious and tender today, for tomorrow I may have to eat them.

Harvest Loaf

Mary Jane Kuepfer - *Chesley, Ontario, Canada*

YIELDS

1 loaf

INGREDIENTS:

1¾ cups flour
1 teaspoon baking soda
1 teaspoon cinnamon
½ teaspoon nutmeg
¼ teaspoon ginger
¼ teaspoon ground cloves
½ cup butter
1 cup sugar
2 eggs
¾ cup pumpkin puree
½ cup chocolate chips
¼ cup raisins or nuts

EQUIPMENT:

Large mixing bowl
Spoon
5x9-inch loaf pan

INSTRUCTIONS:

1. Preheat oven to 350 degrees.

2. In mixing bowl, combine flour, baking soda, cinnamon, nutmeg, ginger, and cloves. Blend in butter, sugar, eggs, and pumpkin. Fold in chocolate chips and raisins or nuts. Pour into greased loaf pan.

3. Bake 60 minutes.

Pumpkin Bread

Katie Yoder - *Fultonville, New York*

YIELDS

3 loaves

INGREDIENTS:

4 eggs
3 cups sugar
2 cups pumpkin puree
⅔ cup water
1 cup olive oil
3½ cups flour
2 teaspoons baking soda
1 teaspoon cinnamon
1 teaspoon nutmeg
½ teaspoon salt
1 cup chopped nuts

EQUIPMENT:

2 large mixing bowls
Spoons
3 loaf pans

INSTRUCTIONS:

1. Preheat oven to 300 degrees.

2. In large bowl, beat eggs. Add sugar, pumpkin, water, and oil, mixing well.

3. In separate bowl, combine flour, baking soda, cinnamon, nutmeg, and salt. Add to first mixture, stirring until well blended. Fold in nuts. Pour into 3 well-greased loaf pans.

4. Bake 1 hour or until done in center.

Note: This bread freezes well.

Zucchini Bread

Esther Burkholder - *Sugarcreek, Ohio*

YIELDS

2 loaves

INGREDIENTS:

1½ cups sugar
3 eggs
1 cup vegetable oil
1 teaspoon cinnamon
1 teaspoon salt
¾ teaspoon baking soda
3 cups flour
2 cups shredded zucchini

EQUIPMENT:

Large mixing bowls
Spoons
2 loaf pans

INSTRUCTIONS:

1. Preheat oven to 325 degrees.

2. In large bowl, blend sugar, eggs, and oil. Add cinnamon, salt, baking soda, and flour. Fold in zucchini until moistened. Divide between 2 greased and floured loaf pans.

3. Bake 1 hour or until done.

Apple Corn Bread

PHEBE PEIGHT - *McVeytown, Pennsylvania*

YIELDS

9 servings

INGREDIENTS:

¾ cup cornmeal

¾ cup spelt or whole wheat flour

3 teaspoons baking powder

¼ teaspoon ground cloves

1 teaspoon cinnamon

¾ teaspoon salt

1 egg, beaten

1 teaspoon vanilla

¾ cup buttermilk

2 tablespoons vegetable oil or butter

1 tablespoon honey

2 cups diced apples

EQUIPMENT:

Sifter

Mixing bowl

Spoon

9x9-inch baking pan

INSTRUCTIONS:

1. Preheat oven to 350 degrees.

2. Sift together cornmeal, flour, baking powder, cloves, cinnamon, and salt in mixing bowl. Add egg, vanilla, and buttermilk. Blend well. Add oil, honey, and apples. Mix thoroughly. Pour into greased 9-inch square pan.

3. Bake 25 minutes.

Cheddar Spoon Bread

Laura Miller - *Fredericktown, Ohio*

YIELDS

6 servings

INGREDIENTS:

2 cups milk, divided
½ cup cornmeal
1 cup shredded cheddar cheese
⅓ cup butter
1 tablespoon sugar
1 teaspoon salt
2 eggs, well beaten

EQUIPMENT:

Medium saucepan
Small bowl
Spoon
1-quart baking dish

INSTRUCTIONS:

1. Preheat oven to 350 degrees.

2. In saucepan, scald 1½ cups milk (heat to 180 degrees).

3. In small bowl, mix cornmeal with remaining ½ cup cold milk and add to hot milk. Cook, stirring constantly, over low heat until thickened, approximately 5 minutes. Add cheese, butter, sugar, and salt. Stir until melted. Remove from heat and stir in eggs. Pour into 1-quart greased baking dish.

4. Bake 35 minutes or until lightly browned and set. Serve immediately.

GREEN PEPPER AND CHEDDAR CORN BREAD

MOLLIE STOLTZFUS - *Charlotte Hall, Maryland*

YIELDS

6 servings

INGREDIENTS:

1 cup finely chopped green pepper

½ cup chopped onion

3 tablespoons butter

1 cup yellow cornmeal

½ teaspoon salt

1 cup plain yogurt

4 teaspoons double-acting baking powder

½ cup butter, melted

2 eggs, well beaten

4 ounces sharp cheddar cheese, finely diced

EQUIPMENT:

Small skillet

Mixing bowl

Spoon

8x8-inch baking dish

Toothpick

INSTRUCTIONS:

1. Preheat oven to 350 degrees.

2. Sauté green pepper and onion in 3 tablespoons butter over medium heat until tender, about 10 minutes, stirring occasionally. Transfer to mixing bowl and add cornmeal, salt, yogurt, baking powder, ½ cup melted butter, eggs, and cheese. Mix just until moistened. Pour into well-buttered 8-inch square baking dish.

3. Bake 25 to 30 minutes or until toothpick inserted in center comes out clean. Serve very hot.

JOHNNY CAKE

MRS. MOSE J. BYLER - *New Wilmington, Pennsylvania*

YIELDS

6 servings

INGREDIENTS:

1 cup cornmeal
1 cup flour
¼ cup sugar
4 teaspoons baking powder
½ teaspoon salt
1 cup milk
1 egg
¼ cup vegetable oil or lard

EQUIPMENT:

Mixing bowl
Spoon
8x8-inch baking pan

INSTRUCTIONS:

1. Preheat oven to 400 degrees.

2. In mixing bowl, combine cornmeal, flour, sugar, baking powder, and salt. Add milk, egg, and oil, and stir only enough to blend. Pour in greased 8x8-inch pan.

3. Bake 20 to 25 minutes.

Light and Tasty Biscuits

Mandy R. Schwartz - *Portland, Indiana*

YIELDS

1 dozen biscuits

INGREDIENTS:

2 cups flour
2½ teaspoons baking powder
½ teaspoon salt
⅓ cup shortening
¾ cup milk
Butter or margarine

EQUIPMENT:

Sifter
Mixing bowl
Fork
Rolling pin
Round biscuit cutter
Baking pan
Pastry brush

INSTRUCTIONS:

1. Preheat oven to 475 degrees.

2. Sift flour, baking powder, and salt into mixing bowl. Cut in shortening with fork until mixture resembles coarse cornmeal. Add milk and blend lightly with fork only until flour is moistened and dough pulls away from sides of bowl.

3. Turn out on lightly floured board. Knead lightly (30 seconds) and roll ¾ inch thick. Cut into biscuit shapes. Place on lightly greased baking pan and brush tops with butter.

4. Bake 12 to 15 minutes.

Melt-in-Your-Mouth Biscuits

Vera Mast - *Kalona, Iowa*

YIELDS

1 dozen biscuits

INGREDIENTS:

2 cups flour
2 teaspoons baking powder
½ teaspoon cream of tartar
½ teaspoon salt
2 tablespoons sugar
½ cup shortening
1 egg
⅔ cup milk

EQUIPMENT:

Sifter
Mixing bowl
Fork or pastry cutter
Spoon
Rolling pin
Round biscuit cutter
Baking sheet

INSTRUCTIONS:

1. Preheat oven to 450 degrees.

2. Sift flour, baking powder, cream of tartar, salt, and sugar into mixing bowl. Cut in shortening. Add egg. Slowly add milk to form sticky dough.

3. Form dough into loose balls and place on baking sheet.

4. Bake 10 to 15 minutes.

Garlic Cheddar Biscuits

Mrs. Reuben Lapp - *Marshall, Indiana*

YIELDS

1 dozen muffins

INGREDIENTS:

1 cup flour

1 tablespoon sugar

2 teaspoons baking powder

½ tablespoon garlic salt or powder, or use fresh ground garlic from your garden

¼ teaspoon salt (or 1 teaspoon if using garlic powder rather than garlic salt)

¼ cup cold butter

1 cup grated cheddar cheese

½ cup milk

EQUIPMENT:

Mixing bowl

Spoon

Baking sheet

INSTRUCTIONS:

1. Preheat oven to 400 degrees.

2. In bowl, mix flour, sugar, baking powder, garlic salt, salt. Add butter, cheese, and milk. Drop by mounds onto baking sheet.

3. Bake 8 to 10 minutes.

Sweet Potato Biscuits

Lorraine Brubacher - *Leonardtown, Maryland*

YIELDS
1 dozen biscuits

INGREDIENTS:
1 cup flour
2 teaspoons baking powder
1 teaspoon salt
½ cup sugar
1 cup mashed sweet potatoes
3 tablespoons shortening
⅓ cup milk

EQUIPMENT:
Mixing bowl
Spoon
Rolling pin
Round biscuit cutter
Baking sheet

INSTRUCTIONS:

1. Preheat oven to 400 degrees.

2. In bowl, mix flour, baking powder, salt, and sugar. Add sweet potatoes. Cut in shortening. Mix in milk to form soft dough. Roll out dough on floured board and cut with cutter. Place on greased baking sheet.

3. Bake 20 minutes.

UNLEAVENED BREAD

MARY SCHWARTZ - *Nottawa, Michigan*

A good bread for Communion

YIELDS
about 100 pieces

INGREDIENTS:
1½ cups flour
¼ teaspoon salt
¼ cup shortening
⅓ to ½ cup milk

EQUIPMENT:
Mixing bowl
Pastry cutter
Spoon
Rolling pin
Fork
2 pancake turners
2 baking sheets
Pizza cutter

INSTRUCTIONS:

1. Preheat oven to 400 degrees.

2. In bowl, mix flour, salt, and shortening with pastry cutter. Add enough milk to make wet dough. Form dough into 2 balls. Roll out one ball of dough to about ⅛-inch thickness. Prick with fork. With 2 pancake turners, transfer dough to slightly greased baking sheet. Cut into small squares with cutter. Roll out second ball and repeat process.

3. Bake 8 minutes.

Note: Do not double recipe. Make a single recipe at a time.

> They baked unleavened cakes of the dough which they brought forth out of Egypt, for it was not leavened; because they were thrust out of Egypt, and could not tarry, neither had they prepared for themselves any victual.
>
> EXODUS 12:39

YEAST BREADS AND ROLLS

Bread is often referred to as a basic food, and if we have just our daily bread and water, we can survive. Bread making is also considered a spiritual practice by some bakers who pray and meditate through the kneading process. No matter how you look at it, the yeasty smell of rising dough is a homey delight in any household.

CHILDREN'S BAG BREAD

LORETTA BRUBAKER - *Farmington, Missouri*

YIELDS
1 loaf

INGREDIENTS:
1 cup whole wheat flour
1 tablespoon salt
1 tablespoon yeast
2 tablespoons vegetable oil
2 tablespoons honey
1 cup warm water
1 cup flour
½ cup whole wheat flour

EQUIPMENT:
Gallon-sized ziplock bag
Towel
Loaf pan

INSTRUCTIONS:

1. Give child gallon-sized ziplock bag. Place in bag 1 cup whole wheat flour, salt, and yeast. Seal bag well and let child gently shake until well mixed.

2. Open bag and add oil, honey, and warm water. Squeeze out as much air as possible and reseal. Have child squeeze bag with hands to mix contents until smooth.

3. Open bag and add 1 cup flour and ½ cup whole wheat flour. Squeeze out as much air as possible and reseal. Have child knead about 10 minutes.

4. Cover bag with towel and let dough rise until doubled.

5. Grease loaf pan. When dough is ready, punch it down, remove from bag, and place in loaf pan.

6. Cover with clean towel and let rise until just above top of pan.

7. Bake 30 minutes at 350 degrees.

Fluffy Wheat Bread for Mixer

Mary Joyce Petersheim - *Fredericktown, Ohio*

YIELDS

2 loaves

INGREDIENTS:

½ cup warm water
1 tablespoon yeast
1 tablespoon sugar
½ teaspoon salt
¼ cup sugar
1 cup warm water
¼ cup lard
1 egg
2 cups whole wheat flour
3 cups bread flour

EQUIPMENT:

Small bowl
Stand mixer
2 loaf pans

INSTRUCTIONS:

1. Mix warm water, yeast, and sugar in small bowl. Set aside for 10 minutes.

2. In mixer bowl, combine salt, sugar, warm water, lard, and egg. Add yeast mixture. Mix briefly. Add whole wheat flour. Mix well. Add bread flour as needed. Mix on low speed until well combined. Let rise 30 minutes.

3. With dough hook, knead for a few minutes. Let rise again until doubled.

4. Shape into 2 loaves. Put in greased pans and let rise.

5. In preheated 325-degree oven, bake 25 minutes or until loaves sound hollow when tapped.

White Bread

Ruby Stoltzfus - *New Holland, Pennsylvania*

YIELDS

4 loaves

INGREDIENTS:

½ cup lukewarm water
2 tablespoons yeast
¼ tablespoon sugar
3 cups lukewarm water
3½ tablespoons lard
½ cup sugar
1½ teaspoons salt
8 cups flour

EQUIPMENT:

Mixing bowl
Spoon
4 loaf pans

INSTRUCTIONS:

1. In mixing bowl, combine lukewarm water, yeast, and ¼ tablespoon sugar. Let sit 15 minutes.

2. Add 3 cups lukewarm water, lard, ½ cup sugar, salt, and flour. Knead until desired consistency. Let rise 45 minutes.

3. Punch down dough and let rise 45 more minutes.

4. Divide into 4 lightly greased loaf pans and let rise but not fill pan.

5. Put in cold oven, turned on to 350 degrees. Loaves will finish rising nicely in oven. Bake 25 minutes or until sides are browned.

100% Organic Whole Grain Bread

Ada J. Mast - *Kalona, Iowa*

A warm slice of this bread with homemade cottage cheese and apple butter is a delicious and nutritious treat. Making it is an overnight process well worth the wait.

YIELDS

2 loaves

INGREDIENTS:

6 cups fresh organic whole grain flour

½ cup organic dairy whey (or water with apple cider vinegar)

1¾ cups water

¾ cup organic butter, lard, or coconut oil

¼ cup warm (100 degrees) water

¼ cup organic raw honey

1½ tablespoons instant yeast

1 tablespoon Himalayan pink salt or Real Salt

¾ teaspoon baking soda

1½ cups organic whole wheat or oat flour

EQUIPMENT:

Mixing bowl

Lid or plastic wrap

Spoon

Glass mixing bowl

2 (5x9-inch) loaf pans

Towel

INSTRUCTIONS:

1. In bowl, mix 6 cups flour, whey, water, and butter. Cover tightly and allow to sit in warm place 8 to 24 hours.

2. The next day, in glass bowl, mix warm water, honey, and yeast. Allow to sit until frothy.

3. Add salt and baking soda to rested flour mixture. Stir well. Add yeast mixture, working yeast throughout flour with your fingers, pulling and stretching to incorporate into lump.

4. When lump begins to form, add 1½ cups flour, ½ cup at a time, while kneading dough on clean surface. A long kneading time of 10 to 15 minutes, leaving dough as sticky as possible, will make the nicest end result. (And it gives you a good workout too!) Cover and let rise in warm place about 2 hours.

5. Punch down dough and shape into 2 loaves. Place in lightly greased loaf pans. Cover again and allow to rise until doubled in volume.

6. Bake in preheated 350-degree oven 35 to 40 minutes. Cool completely before bagging.

GRANDMA'S HONEY WHEAT BREAD

EMMA RABER - *Holmesville, Ohio*

YIELDS

4 large or 5 small loaves

INGREDIENTS:

4 cups warm water

2 heaping tablespoons yeast

1 egg

¾ cup vegetable oil

½ cup honey

½ cup wheat germ

1 tablespoon salt

2 cups whole-wheat flour

9 cups all-purpose flour
(approximately)

EQUIPMENT:

Mixing bowl

Spoon

4 large loaf pans (5 if small)

INSTRUCTIONS:

1. In large mixing bowl, whisk water, yeast, egg, oil, honey, wheat germ, and salt. Add wheat flour first and up to 9 cups all-purpose flour. Let rise until double.

2. Punch down dough and shape into 4 loaves. Place in lightly greased pans. Let rise to double again.

3. Bake in preheated 350-degree oven 50 to 60 minutes.

Cinnamon Raisin Bread

Joann Miller - *Mount Vernon, Ohio*

YIELDS
5 loaves

INGREDIENTS:
⅓ cup vegetable oil
¾ cup sugar
1 tablespoon salt
3¾ cups hot water
1½ cups wheat flour
3 tablespoons yeast
¾ cup oatmeal
1½ cups raisins
7 cups white flour
½ cup sugar
1½ teaspoons cinnamon

EQUIPMENT:
Mixing bowl
Spoon
Small bowl
Rolling pin
5 loaf pans

INSTRUCTIONS:

1. In mixing bowl, combine oil, ¾ cup sugar, salt, and hot water. Add wheat flour and yeast. Add oatmeal, raisins, and white flour. Knead well. Let rise until double.

2. Divide into 5 loaves.

3. In small bowl, mix ½ cup sugar with cinnamon.

4. Roll out dough and sprinkle 2 tablespoons cinnamon-sugar mixture on each loaf. Roll up tight and seal ends. Put in greased pans. Let rise.

5. Bake in preheated 350-degree oven 30 to 35 minutes.

French Bread

Glen Luella Mast - *Topeka, Indiana*

YIELDS

2 loaves

INGREDIENTS:

2 tablespoons yeast
¼ cup sugar
2½ cups warm water
2 teaspoons salt
2 tablespoons vegetable oil
1 teaspoon garlic powder
1 tablespoon Italian seasoning
⅓ cup Parmesan cheese
7 cups flour

EQUIPMENT:

Mixing bowl
Spoon
Baking sheet or 2 loaf pans

INSTRUCTIONS:

1. In large bowl, dissolve yeast and sugar in warm water. Mix in salt, oil, garlic powder, Italian seasoning, and cheese. Slowly add flour and knead a few times. Let rise until doubled.

2. Punch down. Let rise until doubled again.

3. Shape into 2 loaves and place in lightly greased loaf pans.

4. Bake at 350 degrees 18 to 20 minutes.

Grape-Nuts Bread

Katie Shetler - *Fredericksburg, Ohio*

YIELDS

5 loaves

INGREDIENTS:

2 tablespoons yeast
1 teaspoon sugar
1 cup warm water
1½ cups Grape-Nuts cereal
¾ cup sugar
1 tablespoon salt
¾ stick butter
3 cups hot water
2 eggs beaten
4 cups flour

EQUIPMENT:

Small bowl
Large mixing bowl
Spoon
5 small loaf pans

INSTRUCTIONS:

1. In small bowl, combine yeast, 1 teaspoon sugar, and warm water. Stir to dissolve.

2. In large bowl, mix cereal, ¾ cup sugar, salt, butter, and hot water. Cool to lukewarm.

3. Add eggs, yeast mixture, and flour. Let rise 30 minutes to 1 hour.

4. Work down dough, and let rise again.

5. Shape into 5 loaves and place in lightly greased loaf pans. Let rise.

6. Bake in preheated 350-degree oven 30 minutes.

Hillbilly Bread

RUBY BONTRAGER - *Lagrange, Indiana*

Our favorite bread. It stays nice and soft.

YIELDS

6 loaves

INGREDIENTS:

4 cups warm water
1 cup brown sugar
3 tablespoons yeast
4 cups whole wheat flour
6 teaspoons salt
1 cup warm water
1 cup vegetable oil
10 to 11 cups (3½ pounds)
   white flour
Additional oil

EQUIPMENT:

2 large mixing bowls
Spoon
6 (5x9-inch) loaf pans

INSTRUCTIONS:

1. Mix 4 cups warm water with brown sugar, yeast, whole wheat flour, and salt. Let stand 1 hour.

2. Add 1 cup warm water and oil. Work in white flour until dough is well mixed. Grease large bowl and place dough inside, coating with oil. Cover. Let rise 30 minutes.

3. Knead dough. Let rise again for 1 hour. Punch down dough and form 6 loaves.

4. Place loaves in lightly greased bread pans. Let rise until doubled.

5. Bake in preheated 350-degree oven 30 minutes.

OATMEAL BREAD

MRS. HENRY LEID - *Elkton, Kentucky*

YIELDS

4 loaves

INGREDIENTS:

2 cups quick oats
1 cup whole wheat flour
½ cup brown sugar or honey
4 tablespoons butter
2 tablespoons salt
4 cups boiling water
2 tablespoons yeast
1 cup warm water
¼ cup vinegar
12 to 14 cups all-purpose flour

EQUIPMENT:

Large mixing bowl
Spoon
4 (5x9-inch) loaf pans

INSTRUCTIONS:

1. In mixing bowl, combine oats, whole wheat flour, sugar, butter, and salt. Pour boiling water over top and mix well. Cool until lukewarm.

2. Dissolve yeast in 1 cup warm water. Mix into batter along with vinegar and all-purpose flour. Set in warm place and let rise until doubled.

3. Punch down dough and shape into 4 loaves. Place in lightly greased pans.

4. Bake in preheated 350-degree oven 30 minutes or until done.

Favorite Gluten-Free Bread

Maryann Stauffer - *Homer City, Pennsylvania*

YIELDS

2 loaves

INGREDIENTS:

2 cups rice flour

1¾ cups tapioca starch

3½ teaspoons xanthan gum

1½ tablespoons yeast

4 eggs

¼ cup sugar

1 teaspoon salt

2 teaspoons vinegar

¼ cup vegetable oil,
  butter, or lard

1¾ cups warm water

EQUIPMENT:

Small bowl

Large mixing bowl

Spoons

2 loaf pans

INSTRUCTIONS:

1. In small bowl, mix rice flour, tapioca starch, xanthan gum, and yeast. Set aside.

2. In large bowl, beat eggs, sugar, salt, vinegar, oil, and water warm enough to make the full mixture lukewarm. Add flour mixture and stir well for 5 minutes.

3. Put batter into 2 greased loaf pans. Smooth top of batter with wet spatula. Let rise until doubled.

4. Bake in preheated 375-degree oven 40 minutes.

Easy Dinner Rolls

Mary Hoover - *Fortuna, Missouri*

YIELDS

1 dozen rolls

INGREDIENTS:

2 packages dry yeast
¾ cup warm water
⅓ cup sugar
1 teaspoon salt
1 egg, beaten
½ cup butter, melted
3 to 3½ cups flour, divided

EQUIPMENT:

Large mixing bowl
Spoon
9x13-inch pan

INSTRUCTIONS:

1. In large bowl, dissolve yeast in warm water. Add sugar, salt, egg, butter, and 1 cup flour, mixing well. Stir in enough flour to make soft dough. Shape dough into ball. Grease dough, turning to grease all sides. Return dough to bowl. Cover and let rise until doubled.

2. Punch down and shape into 12 balls. Place in lightly greased 9x13-inch pan. Let rise 30 minutes or longer.

3. Bake in preheated 375-degree oven 8 to 12 minutes.

Quick Buttermilk Rolls

Esther L. Miller - *Fredericktown, Ohio*

YIELDS

16 rolls

INGREDIENTS:

¼ teaspoon baking soda
¼ cup sugar
½ teaspoon salt
1 tablespoon yeast
2½ cups flour, divided
1 cup buttermilk
3 tablespoons vegetable oil

EQUIPMENT:

Mixing bowl
Saucepan
Spoons
Rolling pin
Round biscuit cutter
2 (8-inch) round pans

INSTRUCTIONS:

1. In bowl, combine baking soda, sugar, salt, yeast, and 1 cup flour.

2. In saucepan, heat buttermilk and oil until just below boiling or until small bubbles appear around edge of pan. Let milk mixture cool slightly.

3. Add milk to flour mixture and beat well. Stir in remaining flour and knead dough until smooth and elastic, using more flour if needed.

4. Roll out dough to ½ inch thickness and cut into rounds. Place in 2 (8-inch) round pans. Let biscuits rise until doubled in size.

5. Bake in preheated 350-degree oven 10 to 12 minutes or until lightly browned.

Butterhorn Rolls

Iva Yoder - *Goshen, Indiana*

Dough needs to rest overnight.

YIELDS
32 rolls

INGREDIENTS:
1 package yeast
1 tablespoon sugar
3 eggs
1 cup warm water
½ cup sugar
½ cup shortening
½ teaspoon salt
5 cups flour
Melted butter

EQUIPMENT:
Small bowl
Mixing bowl
Spoons
Rolling pin
Pizza cutter
2 to 3 baking sheets
Pastry brush

INSTRUCTIONS:

1. In small bowl, combine yeast and 1 tablespoon sugar.

2. In mixing bowl, beat eggs with warm water. Let stand 15 minutes.

3. To the eggs, add yeast mixture, ½ cup sugar, shortening, salt, and flour. Knead well. Cover and let stand in refrigerator overnight.

4. Next morning, divide dough into 2 parts. Roll out like piecrust in 12-inch circles. With pizza cutter, cut into 16 wedges. Roll up starting with wide end. Let rise 3 to 4 hours.

5. Bake in preheated 400-degree oven 15 minutes or until golden brown.

6. Brush with melted butter. Serve while warm.

7. Can be frozen for later use.

CORNMEAL DINNER ROLLS

PHEBE PEIGHT - *McVeytown, Pennsylvania*

We use this recipe for our wedding reception dinners. The cornmeal mixture gives them a soft texture and pretty golden color.

YIELDS
24 rolls

INGREDIENTS:
⅓ cup cornmeal
½ cup sugar
2 teaspoons salt
½ cup butter
2 cups milk
1 tablespoon yeast
¼ cup warm water
2 eggs, beaten
5 to 6 cups flour
Butter, melted

EQUIPMENT:
Saucepan
Mixing bowl
Spoons
Rolling pin
Biscuit cutter
2 baking sheets
Pastry brush

INSTRUCTIONS:

1. In saucepan, cook cornmeal, sugar, salt, butter, and milk. Remove from heat and cool until lukewarm.

2. In mixing bowl, dissolve yeast in warm water. Add eggs. Combine yeast mixture with cornmeal mixture, stirring well. Add enough flour to form soft dough. Knead in bowl and cover. Let rise until double in size.

3. Punch down. Form into balls for dinner rolls or roll out to 1 inch thickness and cut with biscuit cutter. Place on greased baking sheets. Let rise until almost double in size.

4. Bake in preheated 375-degree oven 15 minutes or until golden. Brush with melted butter.

Grandma's Potato Rolls

Salomie E. Glick - *Howard, Pennsylvania*

YIELDS

1 dozen rolls

INGREDIENTS:

2 cups mashed potatoes
  (may use instant)
5 eggs
1 cup sugar
1 cup vegetable oil
2 packages yeast
2 cups warm water
10 cups bread flour
1 teaspoon salt

EQUIPMENT:

Mixing bowl
Spoons
Small bowl
2 baking sheets

INSTRUCTIONS:

1. In large bowl, combine mashed potatoes, eggs, sugar, and oil.

2. In small bowl, dissolve yeast in warm water. Add to potato mixture and beat well. Add flour and salt. Knead well. Allow to rise.

3. Punch down dough and let rise again.

4. Form into 1½-inch balls. Place on greased baking sheets and allow to rise.

5. Bake in preheated 350-degree oven 10 to 15 minutes until golden brown.

Potato Sourdough Buns

MARIE B. SCHLABACH - *Smicksburg, Pennsylvania*

YIELDS
1 dozen buns

STARTER INGREDIENTS:
1½ cups warm water

1 teaspoon instant yeast

1 cup flour

12 ounces potatoes, cooked and mashed

DOUGH INGREDIENTS:
½ cup warm water

1 egg

2 tablespoons sugar

1 scant tablespoon salt

4 to 4½ cups flour

EQUIPMENT:
Mixing bowl

Wooden spoons

Towel

9x13-inch pan

TO MAKE STARTER:

In bowl, combine water and yeast. Add flour and mashed potatoes. Loosely cover and allow to sit at room temperature at least 8 hours or up to 24 hours before proceeding.

TO MAKE DOUGH:

1. To starter, add water, egg, sugar, salt, and flour, using wooden spoon. Dough should be very soft and slightly sticky. If needed, add a little more flour. Knead 5 minutes. Let rise until doubled.

2. Form balls and flatten into lightly greased 9x13-inch pan. Let rise 45 minutes.

3. Bake in preheated 350-degree oven 15 to 20 minutes.

Sandwich Rolls

Katie Miller - *Arthur, Illinois*

YIELDS

1 dozen rolls

INGREDIENTS:

1 tablespoon yeast
½ cup warm water
1 tablespoon sugar
1 teaspoon baking powder
⅓ cup butter, melted
1 cup milk, scalded
⅓ cup sugar
⅛ teaspoon salt
2 eggs
4½ cups flour

EQUIPMENT:

Small bowl
Mixing bowl
Spoons
2 baking sheets

INSTRUCTIONS:

1. Preheat oven to 425 degrees.

2. In small bowl, dissolve yeast in warm water. Add 1 tablespoon sugar and baking powder. Let stand 20 minutes.

3. In mixing bowl, mix butter, scalded milk, ⅓ cup sugar, and salt. Cool. Add eggs. Add yeast. Work in flour.

4. Divide dough in half. Flatten on 2 baking sheets. Prick dough with fork as you would for piecrust. Cut both sheets into 6 pieces. (I cut lengthwise then in half and 4 crosswise. Buns are approximately 4½x5 inches.)

5. Bake 10 to 12 minutes until lightly golden. Fold each piece in half while still warm.

6. After cooled, fill each sandwich as desired.

BREADSTICKS

DIANA MILLER - *Fredericktown, Ohio*

YIELDS

20 breadsticks

DOUGH INGREDIENTS:

1 tablespoon vegetable oil
2 cups water
1½ teaspoons salt
2 tablespoons sugar
1 tablespoon yeast
4 cups flour

TOPPING INGREDIENTS:

½ cup butter, melted
1 teaspoon garlic powder
2 teaspoons parsley flakes
3 tablespoons Parmesan
  cheese
1 teaspoon Italian seasoning

EQUIPMENT:

Mixing bowl
10x15-inch jelly roll pan

INSTRUCTIONS:

1. Preheat oven to 350 degrees.

2. In bowl, combine oil, water, salt, sugar, and yeast. Work in flour, mixing well. Spread over greased jelly roll pan and let rise 20 to 30 minutes.

3. Spread with melted butter and sprinkle on toppings, then let rise an additional 20 minutes.

4. Bake 15 to 20 minutes. When done, cut into sticks.

Ask God to bless your food, but don't expect Him to make your bread.

Italian Cheese Bread

Valerie Borntrager - *Kalona, Iowa*

YIELDS

about 16 slices

DOUGH INGREDIENTS:

1 cup warm water

1 tablespoon vegetable oil

1 tablespoon yeast

1 teaspoon sugar

1 teaspoon salt

2½ cups flour

TOPPING INGREDIENTS:

¼ cup Italian dressing

¼ teaspoon garlic salt

¼ teaspoon oregano

¼ teaspoon thyme

⅛ teaspoon pepper

½ cup shredded mozzarella cheese

EQUIPMENT:

2 mixing bowls

12-inch pizza pan

Small bowl

TO MAKE DOUGH:

1. In large bowl, mix water, vegetable oil, yeast, sugar, and salt. Add flour and knead until smooth and elastic. Put in greased bowl and let rise 20 minutes.

2. Punch down dough and spread out on 12-inch pizza pan.

TO MAKE TOPPING:

1. Preheat oven to 450 degrees.

2. In small bowl, combine Italian dressing, garlic salt, oregano, thyme, and pepper, and drizzle over dough.

3. Bake 15 minutes.

4. Sprinkle cheese on top and let melt in oven.

5. Serve hot.

Brown Eggs
For Sale
-No Sunday Sales-

BREAKFAST BAKES

*Gathering the whole family around the breakfast
table can often be a challenge, but these baked breakfast
recipes are a good way to serve several people
a nutritious meal all at the same time.*

Breakfast Protein Cookies

Levi D. Stoltzfus - *Willow Hill, Pennsylvania*

YIELDS
12 to 18 cookies

INSTRUCTIONS:
3 large eggs
¾ cup coconut sugar
¼ teaspoon stevia
½ cup coconut oil, melted
1 teaspoon vanilla
1 cup almond, sorghum, or oat flour
⅓ cup coconut flour
½ teaspoon salt
1 teaspoon baking soda
½ cup peanut butter
½ cup dark chocolate chips

EQUIPMENT:
Mixing bowl
Spoon
Baking sheets

INSTRUCTIONS:
1. Preheat oven to 350 degrees.
2. In bowl, blend eggs, sugar, stevia, oil, and vanilla. Add almond flour, coconut flour, salt, and baking soda. Fold in peanut butter then chocolate chips. Let batter sit 10 minutes before baking.
3. Drop by tablespoonfuls on greased baking sheets.
4. Bake 8 to 10 minutes.

GRANOLA CEREAL

LINDA ESH - *Paradise, Pennsylvania*

YIELDS

1 gallon

INGREDIENTS:

4 cups quick rolled oats
8 cups old-fashioned oatmeal
1 cup wheat germ
1 cup flaked coconut
½ cup sunflower seeds
1 cup pecans
1 cup brown sugar
1 teaspoon cinnamon
½ teaspoon salt
1 cup butter
1 cup honey

EQUIPMENT:

Large mixing bowl
Spoons
Saucepan
Baking pan

INSTRUCTIONS:

1. Preheat oven to 325 degrees.

2. Combine rolled oats, oatmeal, wheat germ, coconut, sunflower seeds, and pecans. In saucepan, mix brown sugar, cinnamon, salt, butter, and honey. Heat until melted and well blended. Pour over granola mixture and coat well. Spread in shallow baking pan.

3. Bake 30 minutes or until lightly browned, stirring after 15 minutes.

GRAHAM CRACKER GRANOLA
VERENA WICKEY - *Monroe, Indiana*

YIELDS
almost 1 gallon

INGREDIENTS:
10 cups oats
2 sleeves graham crackers, crushed
1 teaspoon shredded coconut
4 sticks butter
1 cup brown sugar
1 teaspoon salt
2 teaspoons baking soda
1 (12 ounce) package butterscotch chips

EQUIPMENT:
Roasting pan
Saucepan
Spoon

INSTRUCTIONS:

1. Preheat oven to 350 degrees.

2. In large roaster, combine oats, graham crackers, and coconut.

3. In saucepan, melt butter and stir in brown sugar, salt, and baking soda. Pour over dry mixture. Stir well.

4. Bake 1 hour until golden brown, stirring twice.

5. Mix in butterscotch chips while still hot.

Baked Oatmeal

Barbara King - *Paradise, Pennsylvania*

YIELDS

9 to 12 servings

INGREDIENTS:

2 eggs

1 cup sugar

½ cup butter or margarine, melted

3 cups oatmeal

1 cup milk

2 teaspoons baking powder

Pinch salt

EQUIPMENT:

Mixing bowl

Spoon

2-quart baking dish

INSTRUCTIONS:

1. Preheat oven to 350 degrees.

2. Combine eggs, sugar, and butter in mixing bowl. Add oatmeal, milk, baking powder, and salt. Stir until well blended. Spread in buttered 2-quart baking dish.

3. Bake 30 minutes.

4. To serve, add milk or even a scoop of ice cream.

STUFFED FRENCH TOAST

SADIE ANNE KAUFFMAN - *Gordonville, Pennsylvania*

YIELDS

8 servings

INGREDIENTS:

1 loaf homemade bread

2 (8 ounce) packages cream
cheese

12 eggs

2 cups milk

½ cup maple syrup

Cinnamon (optional)

2 cups fresh or frozen berries
(optional for topping)

Chopped nuts (optional for
topping)

EQUIPMENT:

9x13-inch pan

Mixing bowl

Spoon

INSTRUCTIONS:

1. Preheat oven to 350 degrees.

2. Cube bread and place half in 9x13-inch
pan. Cube cream cheese and sprinkle on
top. Add remaining bread cubes.

3. In bowl, beat eggs, milk, and syrup and
pour over bread. Sprinkle with cinnamon,
if desired.

4. Let sit for a while to let bread absorb liquid. Or cover and refrigerate overnight to
bake next morning.

5. Bake 45 minutes or until golden brown.

6. Serve with maple syrup. Top with fruit or
nuts as desired.

Overnight Caramel French Toast

Barbara King - *Paradise, Pennsylvania*

SERVES:

6 to 8

INGREDIENTS:

1 cup brown sugar

½ cup butter

2 tablespoons light corn syrup

12 slices bread

¼ cup sugar

1 teaspoon cinnamon, divided

6 eggs

1½ cups milk

1 teaspoon vanilla

EQUIPMENT:

Small saucepan

Spoons

9x13-inch baking dish

Small bowl

Large bowl

INSTRUCTIONS:

1. In saucepan on medium heat, bring brown sugar, butter, and light corn syrup to a boil. Pour into greased 9x13-inch baking dish. Top with 6 bread slices.

2. In small bowl, combine sugar and ½ teaspoon cinnamon, and sprinkle half over bread. Place remaining bread on top and sprinkle with remaining cinnamon-sugar mixture.

3. In large bowl, beat eggs, milk, vanilla, and remaining ½ teaspoon cinnamon. Pour over bread.

4. Refrigerate overnight.

5. The next morning, bake in preheated 350-degree oven 30 to 35 minutes.

Breakfast Pizza

Mrs. Eli A. Kurtz - *Dayton, Pennsylvania*

YIELDS
8 to 10 servings

CRUST INGREDIENTS:
2 cups flour
½ teaspoon salt
2 teaspoons baking powder
½ teaspoon cream of tartar
½ cup shortening
1 egg
⅔ cup milk

TOPPING INGREDIENTS:
1 pound bulk sausage
1 cup diced, cooked potatoes
2 cups shredded cheese
5 eggs
1 cup milk
½ teaspoon salt
⅛ teaspoon pepper
⅛ teaspoon garlic powder

EQUIPMENT:
2 mixing bowls
Spoons
Large pizza pan with edge or
10x15-inch jelly roll pan
Skillet

TO MAKE CRUST:
1. Preheat oven to 375 degrees.
2. Combine all ingredients in bowl and press into pizza or cake pan.

TO MAKE TOPPING:
1. Brown sausage in skillet. Drain.
2. Spread sausage, potatoes, and cheese over crust.
3. In bowl, beat eggs, milk, salt, pepper, and garlic powder. Pour over crust.
4. Bake 30 minutes.

BISCUITS AND SAUSAGE GRAVY

FREEMAN AND LINDA MILLER - *Spartansburg, Pennsylvania*

YIELDS

6 to 8 servings

BISCUIT INGREDIENTS:

2 cups flour
4 teaspoons baking powder
½ teaspoon cream of tartar
½ teaspoon salt
2 tablespoons sugar
½ cup shortening
1 egg
⅔ cup milk

SAUSAGE GRAVY INGREDIENTS:

1 pound pork sausage
½ cup shortening
⅓ cup flour
4 cups milk
1 can cream of mushroom soup
Salt and pepper to taste

EQUIPMENT:

2 mixing bowls
Fork or pastry cutter
Spoon
Baking sheet
Large skillet

TO MAKE BISCUITS:

1. Preheat oven to 450 degrees.

2. In large bowl, mix flour, baking powder, cream of tartar, salt, and sugar. Cut in shortening until mixture resembles coarse meal.

3. In another bowl, beat egg and milk. Slowly stir into crumbly mixture until just combined. Drop dough onto baking sheet. (Note: Dough can also be gently rolled out and cut with round cutter.)

4. Bake 10 to 15 minutes.

TO MAKE SAUSAGE GRAVY:

1. In large skillet, brown sausage and crumble it. Add shortening, heating until melted. Sprinkle with flour. Stir well. Add milk 1 cup at a time, stirring constantly. Stir in soup. Season with salt and pepper.

2. Serve over warm biscuits.

Simple Cheese Quiche

Martha Beechy - *Butler, Ohio*

YIELDS

6 to 8 servings

INGREDIENTS:

1 unbaked pie shell
5 large eggs, beaten
1 cup milk
1 cup heavy cream
1 teaspoon salt
1 teaspoon pepper
½ cup bacon bits
1 cup shredded cheese

EQUIPMENT:

Pie pan
Mixing bowl
Whisk
Spoon

INSTRUCTIONS:

1. Preheat oven to 350 degrees.

2. Bake pie shell 10 minutes or until lightly browned.

3. In bowl, beat eggs, milk, cream, salt, and pepper until well blended. Stir in bacon bits and cheese. Carefully pour into warm pie shell.

4. Bake 40 to 50 minutes until quiche is light brown.

5. Allow to cool at least 20 minutes before cutting and serving.

Hidden Eggs

Linda Fisher - *Leola, Pennsylvania*

YIELDS

6 servings

INGREDIENTS:

Bread
4 tablespoons butter, melted and divided
6 eggs
Salt and pepper to taste
1 to 2 cups shredded cheddar cheese

EQUIPMENT:

9x9-inch pan

INSTRUCTIONS:

1. Preheat oven to 350 degrees.

2. In 9x9-inch pan, break up enough bread to cover bottom of pan. Drizzle with 2 tablespoons melted butter. Break eggs over bread and sprinkle with salt and pepper. Break up more bread and spread on top of eggs. Drizzle with remaining 2 tablespoons butter and top with shredded cheese.

3. Bake 15 to 20 minutes or until eggs are done.

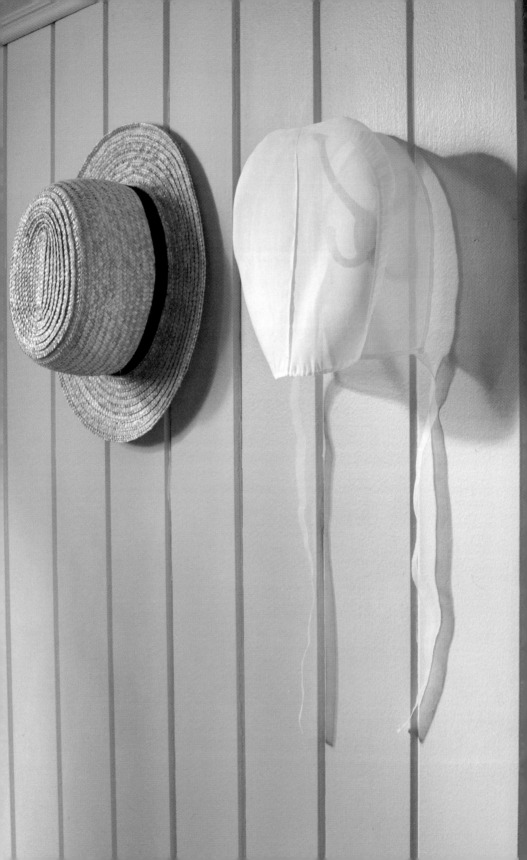

SAVORY BAKES

When it comes to baking, you don't have to stick with sweets alone. Savory bakes are a great addition to the evening meal, bringing warmth and comfort to the family around the supper table.

Sausage Balls

From Amish Cooking Class Cookbook

YIELDS

3 dozen balls

INGREDIENTS:

1 pound ground sausage

3 cups biscuit mix (like Bisquick)

10 ounces grated cheddar cheese

EQUIPMENT:

Skillet

Spoon

Mixing bowl

Baking sheet

INSTRUCTIONS:

1. Preheat oven to 350 degrees.

2. Cook crumbled sausage in skillet. Drain.

3. In mixing bowl, combine sausage with biscuit mix and cheese. Form into balls.

4. Bake about 25 minutes.

Best Pizza Dough

Katie Fisher - *Kirkwood, Pennsylvania*

YIELDS

enough dough for large round pizza or jelly roll pan

INGREDIENTS:

¾ tablespoon yeast

1 cup warm water

1 tablespoon sugar

1 tablespoon vegetable oil

3 cups flour

1 teaspoon garlic salt

1½ teaspoons oregano

EQUIPMENT:

Mixing bowl

Spoon

Large round pizza pan or jelly roll pan

INSTRUCTIONS:

1. Preheat oven to 450 degrees.

2. In mixing bowl, dissolve yeast in water. Add sugar and oil. Add flour, garlic salt, and oregano. Mix well, adding more flour just until dough is no longer sticky.

3. Bake 10 to 15 minutes until golden brown.

4. Add your choice of sauce and toppings, and bake 15 to 20 minutes longer.

WARM GARDEN VEGGIE PIZZA

RHODA TROYER - *Fresno, Ohio*

INGREDIENTS:

Use your favorite pizza crust
3 tablespoons olive oil
½ teaspoon garlic salt
1 teaspoon oregano
1 teaspoon parsley
Pepper slices
Onion slices
Tomato chunks
Cucumber slices
Zucchini slices
Cabbage, cut up
Spinach
Mozzarella cheese, shredded

EQUIPMENT:

Large round pizza or jelly roll
pan
Small bowl
Spoon
Pastry brush

INSTRUCTIONS:

1. Preheat oven to 350 degrees.

2. Mix oil, garlic salt, oregano, and parsley in small bowl. Brush over unbaked pizza crust.

3. Bake 20 minutes.

4. Remove crust from oven and top with vegetables of your choice and cheese.

5. Bake another 15 minutes or until toppings are crisp and hot.

Pizza Pockets

Verna Stutzman - *Navarre, Ohio*

These are good for school lunch boxes.

YIELDS
12 to 14 servings

INGREDIENTS:
Ground beef, sausage, ham, smokies, and/or pepperoni

1½ cups warm water

2 tablespoons yeast

6 tablespoons brown sugar

4½ cups bread flour

Pizza sauce

Shredded cheese

1 teaspoon baking soda

1 cup warm water

Oregano

Butter, melted

EQUIPMENT:
Skillet

Spoon

Mixing bowl

Baking sheet

Pastry brush

INSTRUCTIONS:

1. Brown in skillet any raw meat you plan to use for filling.

2. In mixing bowl, mix 1½ cups warm water, yeast, brown sugar, and flour. Let rise.

3. Preheat oven to 400 degrees.

4. Roll out strips of dough. Put pizza sauce down center of each strip of dough. Top with meat of choice and cheese. Fold both sides of dough strip over center. Pinch to close. Cut off extra dough on ends.

5. In small bowl, dissolve baking soda in 1 cup warm water. Dip pockets in soda water. Place on greased baking sheet and sprinkle with oregano.

6. Bake 20 to 25 minutes until light brown. Brush with melted butter.

Runza Buns

Dorcas Marie Yoder - *Meyersdale, Pennsylvania*

YIELDS
16 servings

DOUGH INGREDIENTS:

1 tablespoon yeast
½ cup warm water
¾ cup lukewarm milk
¼ cup sugar
¼ cup shortening
1 egg
1 teaspoon salt
2 cups whole wheat flour
2 cups flour

FILLING INGREDIENTS:

1½ pounds ground beef
5 cups shredded cabbage
⅔ cup water
½ cup ketchup
¾ cup barbecue sauce
1 teaspoon salt
16 slices cheese

EQUIPMENT:

Mixing bowl
Spoon
Towel
Skillet
Large saucepan
Baking sheet

TO MAKE DOUGH:

In mixing bowl, dissolve yeast in warm water and lukewarm milk. Add sugar and shortening, stirring until melted. Beat in egg and salt. Slowly work in flours. Cover and let dough rise until double in size.

TO MAKE FILLING:

1. In skillet, brown beef and drain grease.
2. In large saucepan, cook cabbage in water 15 minutes; drain. Add beef, ketchup, barbecue sauce, and salt, mixing well.

TO ASSEMBLE:

1. Divide dough into 16 pieces and roll out into 5- to 6-inch circles. Top each circle with cheese slice. Divide filling evenly between circles. Bring edges of dough up over filling to center. Pinch edges to seal. Place seam side down on baking sheet and let rise for about 20 minutes.
2. Bake in preheated 400-degree oven 12 to 15 minutes.

BAKED MACARONI AND CHEESE

JUDY ZIMMERMAN - *East Earl, Pennsylvania*

YIELDS
6 to 8 servings

INGREDIENTS:
3 quarts water
1½ teaspoons salt
8 ounces (2 cups) macaroni
1 teaspoon salt
½ teaspoon dry mustard
¼ teaspoon pepper
8 ounces sharp cheddar
cheese, grated
2 cups milk
4 eggs

EQUIPMENT:
Large pot
Small bowl
Spoon
2-quart casserole dish

INSTRUCTIONS:

1. In pot, bring water and 1½ teaspoons salt to a boil. Add macaroni. Stir to prevent clumping. Simmer 8 minutes.

2. In small bowl, combine 1 teaspoon salt, dry mustard, and pepper.

3. Drain macaroni when cooked. Return to empty pot. Add seasoning mixture, cheese, milk, and eggs. Stir well. Pour into buttered 2-quart casserole

4. Bake in preheated 350-degree oven 1 hour.

Every man should eat and drink, and enjoy the good of all his labour, it is the gift of God.

ECCLESIASTES 3:13

Pizza Bake

Anna M. Byler - *Clymer, Pennsylvania*

YIELDS

8 servings

INGREDIENTS:

1 pound ground beef

½ cup chopped onion

1 pint pizza sauce

1 cup Bisquick baking mix, divided

1½ cups cheese

2 eggs

1 cup milk

EQUIPMENT:

Skillet

Spoon

9x13-inch baking dish

Mixing bowl

INSTRUCTIONS:

1. Preheat oven to 350 degrees.

2. In skillet, brown ground beef and onion. Add pizza sauce and 2 tablespoons of Bisquick. Pour into 9x13-inch pan and top with cheese.

3. In bowl, mix eggs, milk, and remaining Bisquick. Pour on top of first mixture.

4. Bake 30 minutes.

TACO BAKE

Tina Eicher - *Hudson, Kentucky*

YIELDS

8 servings

INGREDIENTS:

2 pounds ground beef

½ package taco seasoning

4 eggs

¾ cup milk

1 cup flour

1 teaspoon baking powder

½ teaspoon salt

1 (10 ounce) can cream of mushroom soup

3 cups chopped lettuce

½ cup chopped green onions

½ cup chopped green pepper

2 cups shredded cheese

EQUIPMENT:

Skillet

9x13-inch baking dish

Mixing bowl

Spoon

INSTRUCTIONS:

1. Preheat oven to 400 degrees.

2. In skillet, brown beef. Drain. Add taco seasoning. Spoon into greased 9x13-inch baking dish.

3. In bowl, beat eggs and milk. Add flour, baking powder, and salt. Pour over meat.

4. Bake uncovered 20 to 25 minutes or until golden brown.

5. Spread mushroom soup on top. Top with lettuce, onions, peppers, and cheese.

CHICKEN PIE

REBEKAH MAST - *Amelia, Virginia*

YIELDS
8 to 10 servings

INGREDIENTS:
2 cups chicken broth

2 tablespoons flour

2 cups diced cooked potatoes

2 cups diced cooked carrots

2 cups cooked peas

2 tablespoons chopped cooked celery

1 small onion, chopped and cooked

2 cups diced cooked chicken

Buttered bread crumbs or pie dough rolled out to fit oblong baking pan

EQUIPMENT:
Saucepan

Spoon

2-quart oblong baking pan

INSTRUCTIONS:
1. Preheat oven to 350 degrees.

2. In saucepan, heat broth. Add 2 tablespoons flour to make thin gravy. Mix with vegetables and chicken. Pour into oblong baking pan and cover with bread crumbs or pie dough.

3. Bake 1 hour.

TOMATO PIE

KATIE FISHER - *Aaronsburg, Pennsylvania*

YIELDS

6 to 8 servings

CRUST INGREDIENTS:

⅓ cup milk

¼ cup vegetable oil

½ teaspoon salt

1 teaspoon baking powder

1 cup flour

FILLING INGREDIENTS:

3 cups peeled, diced fresh tomatoes

½ cup mayonnaise

1 heaping tablespoon brown sugar

1 teaspoon Italian seasoning

Shredded cheese

Diced bell peppers

EQUIPMENT:

2 mixing bowls

9-inch pie pan

Spoon

TO MAKE CRUST:

1. Preheat oven to 375 degrees.

2. In bowl, mix all crust ingredients. Press in bottom and up sides of 9-inch pie pan.

3. Bake 15 minutes.

TO MAKE FILLING:

1. In bowl, combine tomatoes, mayonnaise, brown sugar, and Italian seasoning. Pour in hot crust and top with cheese and bell peppers.

2. Bake an additional 30 minutes.

Corn Pudding

Mary Grace Peachey - *Catlett, Virginia*

YIELDS

8 servings

INGREDIENTS:

3 eggs, beaten
3 cups milk
2 tablespoons sugar
1 teaspoon salt
2 tablespoons butter
½ cup chopped celery
½ cup chopped onion
2 cups corn

EQUIPMENT:

1-quart casserole dish
Spoon

INSTRUCTIONS:

1. Preheat oven to 350 degrees.
2. Combine ingredients in casserole dish
3. Bake 1 hour.

Amish Dressing

B. Saloma D. Yoder - *Mercer, Missouri*

This recipe is often enlarged and served for weddings. Amish housewives memorize this recipe. Often we pressure can the last four ingredients with chicken broth and water to use as a quick starter base for making the dressing.

YIELDS
10 to 12 servings

DRESSING INGREDIENTS:
8 eggs
1 quart milk
1½ teaspoons salt
1 teaspoon chicken base
2 teaspoons parsley flakes
2 cups cubed toasted bread
½ cup cubed cooked chicken
½ cup cubed potatoes
½ cup diced celery
½ cup diced carrots

GRAVY INGREDIENTS:
¼ cup butter
¾ cup flour
Salt and pepper to taste
4 cups water or milk

EQUIPMENT:
Mixing bowl
Spoon
2-quart baking dish
Skillet

TO MAKE DRESSING:

1. Preheat oven to 350 degrees.
2. Beat eggs in mixing bowl. Add milk, salt, chicken base, and parsley. Beat to blend. Add bread, chicken, potatoes, celery, and carrots.
3. Bake in greased 2-quart dish 45 to 50 minutes.
4. Or fry as patties in well-oiled skillet.
5. Serve with gravy.

TO MAKE GRAVY:

In skillet, melt butter; add flour and brown. Season. Add liquid 1 cup at a time. Stir constantly until gravy thickens.

Zucchini Dressing

Rosina Schwartz - *Salem, Indiana*

YIELDS
10 to 12 servings

INGREDIENTS:
1 stick margarine

2 cups coarsely grated zucchini

½ cup chopped onion

3 eggs, beaten

1½ cups cracker crumbs

½ cup shredded cheese

EQUIPMENT:
Large saucepan

Spoon

2-quart baking dish

INSTRUCTIONS:

1. Preheat oven to 350 degrees.

2. Melt margarine in large saucepan. Let cool 5 minutes. Stir in remaining ingredients. Spoon into buttered 2-quart baking dish.

3. Bake uncovered 50 minutes.

CONTRIBUTORS

INDEX OF RECIPES BY SECTION

DESSERTS

PIES

PASTRIES

QUICK BREADS, BISCUITS, AND MUFFINS

YEAST BREADS AND ROLLS

BREAKFAST BAKES

SAVORY BAKES

INDEX OF RECIPES BY KEY INGREDIENTS

OTHER COOKBOOKS BY WANDA AND HER FRIENDS

Wanda E. Brunstetter's Amish Friends Cookbook

Wanda E. Brunstetter's Amish Friends Cookbook: Volume 2

The Best of Amish Friends Cookbook Collection

Wanda E. Brunstetter's Amish Friends Cookbook: Desserts

Wanda E. Brunstetter's Amish Friends Christmas Cookbook

Wanda E. Brunstetter's Amish Friends Harvest Cookbook

Amish Cooking Class Cookbook

Wanda E. Brunstetter's Amish Friends Gatherings Cookbook

Wanda E. Brunstetter's Amish Friends Christmas Cookbook (revised and expanded)

Wanda E. Brunstetter's Amish Friends Farmhouse Favorites Cookbook

Wanda E. Brunstetter's Amish Friends from Scratch Cookbook

Wanda E. Brunstetter's Amish Friends Healthy Options Cookbook